WHAT COMES AFTER PENTECOST?

PRESENTED TO: ______________________________

ON: ______________________________

MESSAGE: ______________________________

____

____

____

____

____

____

____

____

____

____

PRESENTED BY: ______________________________

What Comes After Pentecost?

by Robert B. Thompson

OMEGA Ω Publications
P.O. Box 4130 • Medford, OR 97501

All scripture quotations are taken from the King James Version of the Bible.

WHAT COMES AFTER PENTECOST?

Omega Publications
P.O. Box 4130
Medford, Oregon 97501

Printed in the United States of America
First Printing—June, 1982
Second Printing—June, 1987

ISBN 0-86694-096-0

Contents

Foreword

by Jim McKeever

It is with joy that I write the Foreword for this book, because I think it can be of tremendous help to Christians who want to move deeper into the things of God.

This book is about the Feast of the Tabernacles which was the third, last, and most significant of the three feasts in the Old Testament. Bob Thompson does a beautiful job of showing how to apply the things from the Feast of the Tabernacles to our lives today.

In an introductory way he points out that the first feast, the Feast of Passover, gets applied to our life at salvation. The second feast in the Old Testament is the Feast of Pentecost. This gets applied to a Christian's life when they get filled (baptized) with the Holy Spirit. Unfortunately many Christians who have experienced Pentecost do not know that there is something major beyond Pentecost that God wants them to experience. This book then goes beyond Pentecost into that next realm and shows the individual believers what it is, what it means to them and how they can participate in it.

This third realm could go by a number of different names. In my book *You Can Overcome*, I applied the term "overcomer" to this realm. Bob Thompson uses this term and others to describe this third realm, the realm of the Feast of the Tabernacles. There is much joy and victory and power in this third realm as we move into a deeper and a fuller relationship of God the Father.

I heartily recommend the book, I know that it will be a blessing to you and help you become more like Jesus Christ and enrich your Christian life.

Jim McKeever

Preface

Jim McKeever mentioned to us that there is a current need for a book describing the spiritual fulfillment of the Feast of Tabernacles of the Old Testament. As he was speaking, the thought crossed our mind: How would one go about describing the Pacific Ocean?

When we first received the baptism in the Spirit, in 1948, the Lord gave us burden for the work of Divine grace which comes after the Pentecostal experience. (Pentecost itself was one of the feasts of the Old Testament.)

The burden which the Lord gave in those days came in the context of the Tabernacle of the Congregation, and the seven convocations of the Lord. It was, we believe, a genuine revelation from the Holy Spirit.

The central concept was—and continues to be—Christ *in* you, the hope of glory.

Years passed, occupied mostly by work in public-school education. But the "vision," if we would want to term it that, deepened and enlarged. A picture began to form of the scope of the plan of redemption, as symbolized by the types and shadows of the Old Testament.

It wasn't until 1967, however, that the motivation to write came, catalyzed by a suggestion from Pastor William Pickthorn of Palo Alto, California. After that, the words seemed to flow, perhaps having been formulated unconsciously to a certain extent over the years.

But how does one approach the varied aspects of the New Testament fulfillment of the Feast of Tabernacles—the third great platform of the Christian salvation!

In describing the Pacific Ocean, one would wonder whether to start with its geography, the marine animals and plants, the chemicals found in the water, or its role in the development of California. Like the Pacific Ocean, the Feast of Tabernacles is a majestic, awesome topic.

Inasmuch as we have, during the last decade, written a number of books and booklets on topics associated with the work of grace which follows the new-covenant observance of the Feast of Pentecost, it seemed wise to pull together into one book a compilation of passages dealing with the several dimensions of "Tabernacles."

What is the best way to introduce the Lord's people to the concept that Pentecost is not the last gift of God before Jesus returns?; that there are not only *two* major works of Divine grace (salvation, and the baptism with the Holy Spirit), but *three?;* that there is a definite "more" of Christ for us *before* He comes from Heaven with the saints and holy angels?

Perhaps the introduction could include the fact that the principal types of the Scripture, such as the Tabernacle of the Congregation, the feasts of the Lord, and the journey of Israel from Egypt to Canaan, do not portray two great stages of redemption, but three. It could be added also that an objective view of the present state of the Christian Church, the Body of Christ, will reveal that it has not as yet attained the state of maturity and unity which the Bible sets forth as God's will for the Body, the unblemished wife of the Lamb.

We understand, therefore, that the types predict accurately that which we see to be true. They stipulate that a third major dispensation of grace is required in order to bring the Divine redemption to the perfection declared and prophesied in the holy Scriptures.

The several selections included in our text present some of the issues included in the spiritual fulfillment of Tabernacles. Hopefully, they will serve the saints as an interpretation of those experiences which are coming now to the Lord's people, particularly the Spirit-filled people.

Before we begin the text, it might be helpful to state as clearly and simply as possible what we mean when we speak of a third platform of redemption, as typified by the Levitical Feast of Tabernacles (Leviticus 23:33–43). We will endeavor to sum up the "Pacific Ocean" in a few words.

Deuteronomy 16:16 speaks of the three annual gatherings of the Israelite men: Passover, Pentecost, and Tabernacles.

Passover typifies the basic salvation experience of the blood atonement, repentance and water baptism, and the new spiritual birth.

Pentecost typifies the life lived in the Holy Spirit rather than in the wisdom and energies of the human body and soul.

Tabernacles, including the blowing of Trumpets and the Day of Atonement, typifies the spiritual warfare and judgment which we experience as the Father and the Son make Their abode with us in complete, perfect union.

But doesn't Christ come to live in us when we first are saved?

Yes, He does.

But each of the three areas of redemption has both an immediate fulfillment and a prolonged program.

Salvation takes place the moment we receive Christ by faith. But salvation is a prolonged process, as evidenced by the statement: "he that endureth to the end shall be saved."

Pentecost should be experienced immediately. We should be baptized in water and receive the gift of the Holy Spirit as soon as we repent and place our faith in the Lord Jesus Christ. But beyond all question, learning to walk in the Holy Spirit is a lifelong program.

The *Tabernacles* experience, which is the abiding in us of the Father and Christ, takes place when we are born-again. But being born-again is just that—the beginning of a re-creating of all that we are. As we are being re-created, the Father and the Son increasingly are able to abide in us, as Paul outlined in the last part of the third chapter of Ephesians.

The Scriptures appear to indicate that there will be a specific, historical, Church-wide dimension of the fulfillment of Tabernacles, just as the atonement made by Jesus Christ and the fulfillment of Pentecost were specific historical events. No doubt the historical fulfillment of Tabernacles will put the finishing touches upon the work of redemption, preparing us for the glorious appearing of the Lord Jesus from Heaven.

It may be noticed that we view the blowing of Trumpets,

and the solemn Day of Atonement, as being integral parts of the Feast of Tabernacles.

The Scriptures do not state that these two prior convocations are a part of Tabernacles, and other writers and scholars that we have studied do not group Trumpets and the Day of Atonement with Tabernacles.

Therefore, an explanation of our position may be in order.

First of all, Trumpets and the Day of Atonement *are* considered together, in modern usage, marking the beginning and ending of the "Ten Days of Penitence."

Now, the first day of Tabernacles began only *five* days after the Day of Atonement. Since the Day of Atonement sometimes is considered to be the most important of all of the observances, and yet the name of *Tabernacles* was given to the third great compulsory gathering, it seems probable to us that Trumpets, the Day of Atonement, and Tabernacles should be considered as one great convocation. We think that the Lord intends for the concept to be held in this manner.

Also, the first great annual feast, that of Passover, included the convocation of Firstfruits without mentioning it. Yet, Firstfruits is of the utmost typical importance, its spiritual fulfillment including the resurrection of the Lord Jesus. Jesus Christ rose from the dead on the day of the observance of the covenant of Firstfruits.

In the inclusion of the covenant of Firstfruits, the third of the seven covenants of the Lord, within the first of the three major annual feasts, we have a precedent for including Trumpets and the Day of Atonement, the fifth and sixth of the seven covenants of the Lord, within the third major annual feast.

If Firstfruits was included, but not mentioned, in the first annual gathering, that of Passover, it seems reasonable that Trumpets and the Day of Atonement, because of their calendar proximity to Tabernacles could be considered as being anticipatory of Tabernacles and part of Tabernacles, without violating sane and accepted principles of Biblical interpretation.

It is not likely that the Lord would stipulate three major annual gatherings, and in that stipulation omit one of the events of primary importance—the Day of Atonement!

But it is not these natural features alone which have caused us to include the blowing of Trumpets, and the Day of Atonement, as integral parts of the Feast of Tabernacles. Rather, it is the spiritual fulfillment of the three which, to our way of thinking, emphasizes their interrelatedness and essential unity.

The blowing of Trumpets announces the coming of the Lord and the resurrection of the dead.

The Day of Atonement is the reconciliation of man with God which must take place when the Lord comes to live with man.

The Feast of Tabernacles is that eternal union which God in Christ is seeking with man—a union which can be based only upon complete and perfect reconciliation.

It can be seen from the above that the three final convocations of the Lord must be considered together. It is impossible to have a "Tabernacles" experience until the Lord has come and cleansed His Temple in the "Day of Atonement." For this reason we include Trumpets and the Day of Atonement as being inseparable elements of the Feast of Tabernacles.

Today many of the saints are seeking power. They desire power with God.

But the goal of the true Christian should not be power with God; it is union with God through Jesus Christ. And union with God is possible only as we allow the Lord to purge us, in fulfillment of the Day of Atonement, from all sin and self-seeking.

Why don't you, dear reader, come with us as we take our journey up from Sinai (Pentecost) and march toward the land of promise! A deeper judgment and reconciliation to God will prepare us for the fullness of God's glory promised in both the Old Testament and the New Testament.

Robert B. Thompson
Escondido, California

PART I

THE THREE FEASTS OF THE LORD

1

The Three Feasts

What can we expect after we have experienced Pentecost?

Toward *what* do we press after Pentecost, after we receive the baptism in the Holy Spirit?

Under Moses the Jews were given seven holy convocations to observe annually. Do you know what they were? Do you know how they apply to our Christian walk?

Pentecost was the fourth observance. Have you been as far as Pentecost? There were three convocations *after* Pentecost, showing us that the Lord has more for us. Christ does not want us to stop at Pentecost!

THE FEASTS OF THE LORD

We should first briefly review the feasts of the Old Testament. These feasts are dealt with extensively in a book by the author entitled *The Feasts of the Lord,* published by Omega Publications (P.O. Box 4130, Medford, Oregon 97501). If one wishes to pursue this topic, I would refer them to that work. Now for a summary of these feasts.

The feasts of the Lord are one of the major types of the Scriptures. They portray the scope of the plan of salvation, guiding and encouraging us as we move on with the Holy Spirit to the rest of God, to the Feast of Tabernacles, to the fullness of the salvation which is in Christ Jesus.

2 And the Lord spake unto me, saying,

3 Ye have compassed this mountain long enough: turn you northward.

—Deuteronomy 2

9 There remaineth therefore a rest to the people of God.
—Hebrews 4

The Levitical convocations are listed in the twenty-third chapter of the Book of Leviticus in the Old Testament. There are seven of them. Sometimes they are called the *Levitical feasts,* or the *feasts of the Lord.* But in actuality they were not all feasts, as we think of the word *feast.*

However, they were all *convocations,* that is, observances in which the people of Israel were called together by the Lord.

Two Guidelines for Interpreting Bible Types

Before we go further, let us mention two rules for interpreting Bible symbols, or *types,* as they are called. Types, such as the seven convocations of Israel, help us understand the Lord Jesus and His plan of salvation.

The first rule of interpretation is this: study the symbol, and then ask the Holy Spirit to cause the main truth to rise to the surface. Do not attempt to carry every aspect of the symbol through to its logical conclusion—logical according to the reasoning of the human mind.

The Holy Spirit *always* interprets His own statements and illustrations!

We see truth through a glass darkly, as Paul mentions in I Corinthians, Chapter 13. The Holy Spirit must be the One Who throws light on the passage of Scripture we are studying. Usually a type presents one truth, or line of truth, and the Spirit will give us the understanding.

For example, Christ is the *Lamb* of God. The truth which rises to the surface is that Christ was led away as an offering for our sins, and that we eat His body and drink His precious blood as our Passover.

But we cannot pursue the symbol further and claim that Christ today is led around helplessly and is a prey for every wolf that appears on the scene!

Again, in one setting leaven is a type of sin. In another setting, leaven is a type of the Kingdom of Heaven. There is a flexibility of application here, showing us that we must not create a rigid system of interpretation of the Bible based upon types. If we do, we will miss the point of what the Holy Spirit is revealing to us.

Still another example is this: the Christian Church is referred to as the bride of the Lamb. The symbol of marriage indicates to us that we are to enter into spiritual union with Christ and become one with Him. But we can't go on from this and state that Christians are feminine because they are termed the "bride," and that the bride is a different group from the sons of God who are male because they are "sons."

Every aspect and detail of a Bible type, or parable, does not reveal spiritual truth!

The second guideline for interpreting Bible symbols is this: all interpretation of symbols must be taught directly in the New Testament.

For example, repentance from our sinful ways is portrayed by the removal of leaven during the convocation of Unleavened Bread. The New Testament directly teaches us to get rid of sin. First, there is the bringing down to death of our first personality through entering into the death of Christ upon the cross, and the rising up of the new sin-free personality through entering into the resurrection of Christ. This death and resurrection is represented as we are baptized in water.

Second, we have the provision of confessing and receiving cleansing from the sins which we practice as Christians, as taught in I John 1:7–9.

If we claim that the putting away of leaven during the convocation of Unleavened Bread portrays the putting away of sin from the Christian, we must be able to turn to the New Testament and find written there that God indeed has provided grace through the Lord Jesus Christ to enable us to put sin out of our life.

Christ has made it possible for us to put away the old leaven of the world, of Satan, and of our own pride and lust of the flesh.

If we are to make a success of interpreting Bible types we should look to the Holy Spirit for the main idea and not attempt to force an interpretation which doesn't fit, or press too hard on the details.

Also, there must be direct New Testament teaching for whatever applications we make.

ENUMERATION OF THE SEVEN LEVITICAL CONVOCATIONS

1. *Passover*—In the fourteenth day of the first month at even is the Lord's passover (Leviticus 23:5).
2. *Unleavened Bread*—And on the fifteenth day of the same month is the feast of unleavened bread unto the Lord; seven days ye must eat unleavened bread (Leviticus 23:6).
3. *Firstfruits*—Speak unto the children of Israel, and say unto them, When ye be come into the land which I give unto you, and shall reap the harvest thereof, then ye shall bring a sheaf of the firstfruits of your harvest unto the priest (Leviticus 23:10).
4. *Pentecost*—And ye shall count unto you from the morrow after the sabbath, from the day that ye brought the sheaf of the wave offering; seven sabbaths shall be complete: even unto the morrow after the seventh sabbath shall ye number fifty days; and ye shall offer a new meat offering unto the Lord (Leviticus 23:15, 16).

The term *Pentecost* refers to the Greek word which has to do with the number *fifty*. The Feast of Pentecost derives its name from the fact that it was celebrated fifty days from the convocation of Firstfruits.

Sometimes the Bible uses the name "feast of weeks" for the Feast of Pentecost.

5. *Trumpets*—Speak unto the children of Israel, saying, in the seventh month, in the first day of the month, shall ye have a sabbath, a memorial of blowing of trumpets, a holy convocation (Leviticus 23:24).
6. *Day of Atonement*—Also on the tenth day of this seventh month there shall be a day of atonement: it shall be a holy convocation unto you; and ye shall afflict

your souls, and offer an offering made by fire unto the Lord (Leviticus 23:27).

7. *Tabernacles*—Speak unto the children of Israel, saying, The fifteenth day of this seventh month shall be the feast of tabernacles for seven days unto the Lord (Leviticus 23:34).

SEVEN CONVOCATIONS GROUPED INTO THREE FEASTS

The seven convocations of Israel were grouped into three great annual observances:

> **16 Three times in a year shall all thy males appear before the LORD thy God in the place which he shall choose; in the feast of unleavened bread, and in the feast of weeks, and in the feast of tabernacles: and they shall not appear before the LORD empty:**
>
> **17 Every man *shall give* as he is able, according to the blessing of the LORD thy God which he hath given thee.**
>
> **—Deuteronomy 16**

The above are the three holy feasts which occurred annually. Passover, Unleavened Bread, and Firstfruits were termed the Feast of *Unleavened Bread.* Pentecost was termed the Feast of *Weeks.* Trumpets, the Day of Atonement, and Tabernacles were termed the Feast of *Tabernacles.*

Every Hebrew male without exception was to appear before the Lord three times in the year. He was to come with something in his hand to give unto the Lord: an animal from his flock or herd; some oil or wine; some grain or money—something taken out from the riches with which God had blessed him.

The Feast of Passover, consisting of Passover, Unleavened Bread, and Firstfruits, occurred in March-April of our calendar. These three ceremonies suggest to us the first aspect of the process of Divine redemption—that of accepting the Passover blood; repenting and entering into water baptism for the washing away of our sins; and the born-again experience of being made alive by the Spirit of God and having Christ born in us.

The Feast of Pentecost, occurring approximately in May of our calendar, brings to mind the experience of the baptism of the Holy Spirit which causes us to grow strong in Christ; bear witness in power; lead a holy life; worship God in Spirit-filled adoration; be ministered to and minister; and serve as a priest of God by bringing the blessings of Christ to the peoples of the earth.

The Feast of Tabernacles, consisting of Trumpets, the Day of Atonement, the seven days of the week of Tabernacles, and the high Sabbath of the eighth day, took place in September–October of our calendar.

The convocation of Trumpets speaks to us of God's New Year's Day; of war; of rejoicing; of the redemption of the Year of Jubilee; of victory; and of the redemption of our mortal body which will accompany the glorious appearing of our Lord Jesus Christ from Heaven with the saints and holy angels.

The Day of Atonement calls to mind our continuing need to bring our sins to Christ for forgiveness and cleansing under the guidance of the Holy Spirit. Tabernacles portrays to us the coming of the Father and the Son to dwell in us forever; and of the new heaven and earth reign of Jesus Christ.

The eighth day of Tabernacles is the first day of the new week of eternity—the week which has no end. Complete fulfillment of the eighth day occurs during the new heaven and earth reign of Christ. The beginning of the fulfillment takes place at the moment of our believing in Jesus Christ: "I am the resurrection, and the life: he that believeth in me, though he were dead, yet shall he live: and whosoever liveth and believeth in me shall never die" (John 11:25, 26).

In terms of our present calendar, the three annual celebrations were arranged as follows:

1. Passover 2. Unleavened Bread 3. Firstfruits	— *Feast of Passover*	(March)
4. Pentecost	— *Feast of Pentecost (or Weeks)*	(May)

5. Trumpets
6. Day of Atonement — *Feast of Tabernacles* (September)
7. Tabernacles

These three feasts speak of many wonderful things. One of these things is the three areas of redemption.

2

The Three Areas of Redemption

There are three major phases of the redemption which is in Christ Jesus. These three phases are not like three rungs on a ladder which we are to climb, or three grades in school which we are to attain. Rather, the three phases are as three facets of one diamond. They are three dimensions of the one redemption.

When we have the Lord Jesus Christ, upon accepting Him as our personal Savior and Lord, we possess the entire and whole redemption which God has provided. Yet, there are three major aspects of the Divinely-given redemption, and the Scripture alludes to them in several different ways.

The three principal Levitical feasts typify the three aspects of the plan of redemption in Christ.

In addition, there are several other Scripture references which enable us to gain insight into the areas of redemption:

1. The Outer Court, Holy Place, and Holy of Holies of the Tabernacle of the Congregation (Exodus 40:18–30).
2. The three great divisions of the journey of the Israelites, which were the exodus from Egypt, the wilderness wandering, and the entrance into the land of promise.
3. The water to the ankles, knees, and loins (Ezekiel 47:3–5).
4. The hundredfold, sixtyfold, and thirtyfold (Matthew 13:8).
5. The fruit, more fruit, and much fruit (John 15:2–5).
6. The three stories of Noah's Ark (Genesis 6:16).
7. The three means of overcoming (Revelation 12:11).

8. The three "days" (Hosea 6:2; Luke 13:32).
9. The manifestation of Christ's glory upon the third day (John 2:1–11).
10. The three temptations of Christ (Luke 4:1–13).
11. Christ rose from the dead on the third day! (Luke 24:6).

Be alert, as you study the Bible, for events which had to do with a three-day period of time (Joshua 1:11; Nehemiah 2:11; Exodus 19:15; Jonah 1:17; and so forth).

These dissimilar and widely scattered examples may seem to be unrelated, at first glance, and their "threeness" coincidental. But a closer look may show that each example is portraying much the same thing and yields understanding of the meaning of the redemption which is in Christ.

Paul speaks of being "caught up to the third heaven" (II Corinthians 12:2), and so it appears that there are at least three heavens. And since Hebrews 9:21–24 informs us that the Tabernacle and its vessels were "patterns of things in the heavens," we might conclude that Heaven itself is in three divisions and that we can learn a great deal about the redemption which comes to us from Heaven by studying the Old Testament types, and also by meditating upon what Christ has done and is doing in the earth.

The redemption which is in Christ Jesus is a mighty work, a broad work, a perfect work. It includes the growth of the believer to maturity; the growth of the Church, the Body of Christ, to unity and maturity; and also the setting up of the Kingdom of God upon the earth.

The believer is "born again" into the Kingdom of God. The believer is baptized by the Holy Spirit into the Church, the Body of Christ. The believer fights his way, through the wisdom and power which the Holy Spirit gives, into the "throne" phase of redemption. He must "overcome" if he is to rule with Christ (Revelation 3:21).

But it is one redemption, one Lord Jesus Christ, one precious blood of the Lamb of God, one Holy Spirit, one Body of Christ, one eternal life, one Kingdom of God, one God the

Father of Whom and through Whom are all aspects of the one redemption.

In order to enter into each of the three areas of redemption we must die the death which God has ordained. If we are willing to go through the "deaths" which God has decreed, then we will receive the accompanying resurrections. The deaths are just that–deaths! But the resurrections are so glorious that the deaths are soon forgotten.

"No man can see God and live"! Therefore, we die that we might live eternally in His Presence.

It is our understanding that the greatest of all revivals to date is now underway in the Church. It may be true that the third death which we will be describing, through the help which the Spirit gives, has never before been experienced by the churches to any great extent. Yet, this third death will be the one which will bring us into the total authority and power which Jesus has promised to the Church.

The doctrine which the Holy Spirit is giving to us in these days is not new. Rather, it is apostolic. It has been in the Scriptures since they were written. There have been many outstanding saints who have pressed into close fellowship and union with God through Christ. But God, since the days of the revival under Martin Luther, has been increasing the understanding of the Church as a whole.

We have been in a period of restoration for the past several hundred years. If we will allow the Holy Spirit to teach us, the doctrines of the Lord Jesus are simple, clear, and bring peace and joy to our hearts. Sometimes the outworking of them in our lives involves of necessity a fiery trial for a season.

SALVATION: THE FIRST AREA OF REDEMPTION

The first area of redemption is that of salvation. The call of the evangelist is that people might receive salvation. What does it mean to be *saved?* It means to possess God's guarantee that when the Day of Wrath comes–and it surely is coming!–the believer will be kept from destruction by the power of God.

God is coming to the earth to judge the works of men and

devils. The judgment which is just over the horizon is unspeakably terrible. People today have talked themselves into the belief that God is a kindly old gentleman who can do neither good nor harm. But Paul says, "knowing therefore the terror of the Lord, we persuade men" (II Corinthians 5:11). We Christians need to gain some idea of the terror of the Lord before we can really appreciate what it means to be saved from wrath.

Christ came to seek and to save those who are lost. If any person, young or old, will receive Him by faith and hold that faith throughout life, he or she will be saved in the Day of the Lord. He who endures to the end will be saved. Some will gain an abundant entrance into the Kingdom of Christ, while others will be saved "yet so as by fire."

Perhaps you as an individual are not making a great success of the Christian life, at least not in your own opinion. But if you will keep your hope steadfast in the Savior and not turn your heart away from Him in discouragement, pride, lust, or rebellion, you will be saved in that Day of reckoning.

The next coming of Christ will be so frightful that no words of ours can protray adequately what the world is about to face. The most terrifying scene which ever before has appeared upon the earth will seem like child's play when compared with the wrath of God which is going to be poured out under the administration of Christ and His saints.

The blood of Christ is a protection over us and our household when God passes over the earth to judge the gods of this world. Let us make sure that we are under the protection of the "Passover" blood in that Day which is at hand.

After the Millennium comes the Lake of Fire. The Lake of Fire is no mere symbol of God's anger. It is a real lake, a place of eternal torment. It is reserved for the devil and his angels, and for all others who reject the lordship of Jesus Christ.

Make no mistake! There is a lake which burns with the pungent smell of burning sulfur. There will be devils and people in it. We do not want to be cast into the Lake of Fire. We desire to be saved from it.

In Christ is salvation in the Day of God's wrath. Let us not neglect this salvation; rather, let us embrace it and preach it.

It is God's gift freely given, the sacrifice of God's only-begotten Son. We do not want to be numbered among those who reject God and His Gift. Let us receive Christ and be saved.

Heaven is a real place, a paradise of peace and joy. Heaven is the most wonderful dreams of people in solid and enduring form. To be received into Heaven when we die requires accepting Christ in obedience to the will of God. "Believe on the Lord Jesus Christ, and thou shalt be saved, and thy house." "He that believeth and is baptized shall be saved."

Each person who receives Jesus Christ as Savior and Lord is at once redeemed from the authority, guilt, and death of sin. By *death,* in this instance, we mean separation from the Presence and acceptance of God.

Each human being is born in sin, because of the transgression of Adam and Eve. We all have an inborn tendency toward moral corruption. We sin because it is our nature to do so. There is no way in which we can redeem ourselves. We do not possess the price to pay God for past transgressions and we do not have the power to quit sinning now. We must have a redeemer!

The root of our problem is Satan and the rebellion in Heaven. That is where sin began. Sin was introduced into the garden by the serpent, not by our ancestors, Adam and Eve. Therefore, God has determined to judge and bring to an end the entire first creation, and to punish those angels who rebelled against Him.

We are not to attempt to please God by our own wisdom and strength. God has a master plan, and we can enjoy perfect peace and rest only as long as we are willing to fit into God's design for our own individual life.

Jesus Christ bore upon Himself the sins of the whole world. The judgment of God came upon Christ and He was crucified. In Christ, God brought to an end the first creation. In Christ, God brought judgment upon the evil lords of darkness and completely destroyed their authority and power. God in Christ overcame Satan.

All of that was accomplished upon the cross of Calvary. We had nothing to do with it. The Divine redemption has to do with God's wrath, God's law, God's righteousness, God's provision, God's Nature and program. All we can do is accept it and cooperate with it.

When we come to Christ, God directs us to be baptized in water. "Go down into the water," God commands, "showing that you are willing to die to your first life—to the first creation. Accept My judgment upon the source of sin in your life. Take your forgiveness by faith and be believing and thankful. It is My free gift to you."

And so by faith we establish that our "old man," our first personality, is now dead through our participation with Christ upon the cross. We count that our sinful nature is being destroyed, its authority over us having been completely removed in Christ. We declare in militant faith that our new inner man, the new life which has been born again in Christ, is now risen with Christ.

We understand from the Scripture that the new life which we possess is without condemnation from any source. We are free from all guilt. Every "Egyptian" died in the Red Sea, so to speak, as demonstrated through baptism in water. Through means of the death of our old personality we are free to be married to the Lord Jesus Christ.

At the moment of our receiving Christ we receive perfect redemption through means of the payment of the blood of the Lamb of God. The life's blood of Christ, God's Lamb, paid for our deliverance. We go free. The first creation came to an end upon the cross. The believer in Christ comes up from the waters of baptism free from condemnation, having been forgiven every sin through the redemption which God has provided.

Salvation is a first reaping of our life. It is a reaping unto Christ. It is an instant death by faith, potentially destroying the ability of our old nature, and sin, to dominate us.

We say *potentially,* because the actual destruction of sin and the transformation of our personalities depend upon the working out in hope, faith, and obedience that which God and we declared to be true in our baptisms in water. Water baptism portrays that which will become a fact, if we follow Christ faithfully: the death of our first personality and the creation of a new personality. And our new life is raised up to be hidden with Christ in God (Colossians 3:1–4).

The very righteousness of Jesus Christ Himself is imputed to us—freely given to us. It is the grace of God in action. We now are without condemnation and are invited and welcomed to enter boldly into the Holy of Holies in Heaven before the Father, there to make our needs and desires known to Him Who sits upon the throne of the universe.

We are accepted in the beloved Son, Jesus Christ. The holy angels rejoice and the bells of Heaven ring because a prodigal son has returned to the Father's house. From now on, death holds no terror for us. When we die we go straight to Heaven and dwell forevermore with God and the Lamb, and with the saints and angels.

We were dead spiritually, being cut off from God. But now, by means of the atonement made through the blood of the righteous Jesus, we are accepted of God. God's Holy Spirit takes up His abode in us. The Spirit of God is eternal life within us, the pledge of the more complete redemption yet to come. All past transgressions are forgiven. The covering of the "Passover" blood shields us from the wrath of God.

In the preceding paragraphs we have described the *salvation* phase of Christianity. Every person who would have eternal life must begin here. We must receive Christ personally as Lord and Savior and be baptized in water. Upon doing this we are "born again."

The only way a man, woman, boy or girl can enter into the Kingdom of God is by being born again. Until a person is born again he can neither see nor enter the Kingdom of God. Our death with Christ upon the cross and our new birth into the Kingdom of God are the first area of redemption.

SANCTIFICATION: THE SECOND AREA OF REDEMPTION

The first area of redemption, as we have said, is that of salvation, of acceptance by the Lord, of passing from death unto life, of remission of the guilt of past sin through means of the blood of Christ. The grace of God is given freely to us through Christ Jesus and we are received as a child of God.

The second area of redemption is that of sanctification. By *sanctification* is meant the setting apart of the Christian as holy unto the Lord. It appears that a great many Christians have had a genuine experience of salvation but have stopped there. They have never cooperated with the Holy Spirit in the task of directing their daily behavior into ways pleasing to the Lord Jesus.

In the first area of redemption, that of initial salvation, we die unto the world and are raised in Christ Jesus. In the second area of redemption, that of sanctification, we die unto the works of the flesh, the carnal nature, and are raised up into the life lived in the wisdom and power of the Holy Spirit.

> **4 That the righteousness of the law might be fulfilled in us, who walk not after the flesh, but after the Spirit.**
> **5 For they that are after the flesh do mind the things of the flesh; but they that are after the Spirit the things of the Spirit.**
> **—Romans 8**

The second area is the area of the testimony; the area of the Holy Spirit. The Holy Spirit predominates in this area as He leads us, instructs us, builds us up in preparation for our presentation to the Lord Jesus Christ as the glorious Church without spot or wrinkle. The area of sanctification is one of conquering sin; of instruction in godliness; of the testimony of the Person, will, and way of God Almighty; of preparation for greater transformation and blessings yet to come.

The Holy Spirit enables us to live by the Scriptures and to bring people to the Savior. The Holy Spirit leads us as we share with others our personal experiences with Christ. He imparts unto us gifts and ministries. Through the anointing of the Spirit, the Word of Christ is confirmed with mighty signs and wonders.

The Holy Spirit works night and day forming Christ in us. He intends to bring us into the image of Jesus Christ and into perfect oneness in and with Christ. If we will cooperate with Him, He will set us apart each day as holy unto the Lord. He is the *Holy* Spirit.

It is the will of Christ that the members of the Body of Christ begin to follow the Holy Spirit into the putting to death of the deeds of the body (Romans 8:13). If the Holy Spirit is not leading us into the conquest of the deeds of our flesh, then we are not sons of God. No person walks in peace and fellowship with Christ Jesus and continues in known sin.

Although our deliverance from the bondages of the flesh takes a while to accomplish—we are not delivered into sinless perfection overnight!—yet our redemption in this area is as definite, as real, as certain, as is our initial step of salvation. The entire Book of I John holds forth the thesis that Christians are not to continue in sin; that whoever is continuing to sin is not walking in Christ and has neither seen Him nor known Him.

In times past we have not understood how to overcome our sinning, and so we have put our trust in Christ and have left the problem with Him. But now He is showing us that if we will allow the Holy Spirit to do so, the Spirit will enable us to wash our robes in the blood of the Lamb, thus becoming sparkling white in the righteous conduct which God requires.

We must learn to judge ourselves through the Holy Spirit. Little by little we achieve the victory of sanctification of spirit, of soul, of body. In this manner we purify ourselves in preparation for His glorious appearing (I John 3:1–3).

We might say that the area of sanctification is a reaping unto the Holy Spirit, just as the area of initial salvation is a reaping unto Christ. Of course, we are not attempting to set forth new doctrine or an inflexible concept. The Father, Son and Holy Spirit always work together in all aspects of our redemption. Nevertheless, our division into these three areas of redemption may be helpful to us as we ponder the meaning of redemption and atonement.

In sanctification we become dead to the life lived in the impulses of the flesh and mind. By the power which the Holy Spirit provides we are raised up into freedom from the need to keep on serving the lusts of the flesh and of the eyes.

The second area of redemption is a place of wilderness wandering, of learning the ways of God, of coming under God's law of the Spirit of life, of Christ pruning back the fruit of one's life and the bearing of more fruit, of daily manna from the Lord.

In the area of sanctification, the Church begins to be

formed into an army, and also moves toward maturity as the Servant of the Lord (Isaiah, Chapter 42). But the fullness of the development of God's warriors and servants takes place in the third area—that of *conquest*.

In the first area, salvation, we Christians are so occupied with what we are receiving from God that not too much is accomplished from the standpoint of what we are going to return to God in the way of service. But growth in service comes to us if we follow on to know the Lord. We begin to exercise a priestly role as we learn more about how to please the Lord and serve Him.

To get over into the spiritual side of things for a bit, it appears that the second area of redemption has to do with the second level of Heaven. The first level of Heaven is the place where we are accepted of God and enjoy the love, joy, and peace which follow acceptance by Him.

The second level of Heaven seems to be the place where we minister before God as a prophet and priest, through means of the ministries and gifts of the Holy Spirit. The third level is that of the throne of God and of the Lamb. The third level is the area in which we rule in Christ with great authority and power.

Before Adam and Eve rebelled against the Word of God, the material creation was alive through means of the blending of the spiritual realm with the natural realm—the condition which would be true today if the earth had not been placed under the curse of God. Unfortunately, Satan entered into Eden, and Adam and Eve were no match for his wiles. Heaven withdrew from the earth and God placed cherubim to guard the way to the tree of life.

When we Christians die we enter into the peace and joy of Heaven, the blessed condition which was true upon the earth before sin entered in. Heaven is a real place, and what a time of joy and peace we will experience when we meet our loved ones there and enjoy the goodness of Christ!

The third level of Heaven, that which Paul apparently visited in a vision, or perhaps in reality, is the throne of God. Paul refers to the third Heaven as *Paradise* (II Corinthians 12:4). God's will is done at this high level of government and authority. The third level of Heaven corresponds to the third area of redemption. If we are faithful in overcoming, Jesus has promised us that we will be lifted up to be seated with Him upon the throne of glory.

Spiritual warfare rages about us as we press on past initial salvation into the fullness of sanctification and victory. There yet is much evil in the churches—sometimes more than is found in the world! It may be recalled that when Pilate was faced with the Lord Jesus Christ he wanted to release Him. But Pilate was prevented from doing so by the priests of Israel.

The Jewish leaders howled for Christ's blood. Here is Satan working in a religious setting. Pilate represents the world. The leaders of Israel represent religious activity and church government. Do you see that when the world would have set Christ free, the church leaders demanded that He be crucified? Here is an example of the problems of rebellion and self-will which exist at the second level, the level of ministry and church activity.

Today the world is evil and growing worse all the time. There is Satanic activity in the world and abominations are being committed. But when Christ begins to pour out His Spirit in these last days, it may be true that there will be persecution from the churches as well as from the world. In the last days Satan will be cast out of Heaven into the earth, and his thrashings about in the earth will be expressed both in the world and also in the religious organizations.

The battle against sin, against the kingdom of darkness, is taking place in every true believer in Christ. The battle against sin cannot be waged successfully in the world, because the world is dead in sin. But the Holy Spirit of God is dwelling eternally in the believers in Christ. Therefore, in them there is a struggle going on night and day.

Satan is striving to maintain his hold over the conduct of each Christian. The Holy Spirit in each Christian is striving to bring him or her into deliverance from having to obey the spirit of the world, Satan, and the carnal nature. Also, his or her self-will and self-love is in the process of being "crucified."

Those Christians who are pressing forward in the Lord Jesus Christ are gaining the upper hand over sin. But total victory takes a while to accomplish! However, the Lord God of Heaven has promised that He will deliver even the lords of darkness into our hands and that we will destroy them with total destruction until they have been consumed (Deuteronomy 7:23).

Through the wisdom and power of Christ, and in His time, we will be able to tear down the strongholds of Satan in the heavenlies. Every spirit is going to be brought under the feet of Jesus Christ. Christ is going to use the members of His Body to crush the evil armies of wickedness (Romans 16:20).

When a Christian confesses a sin and gains victory over that sin through the authority of the blood of Christ and the power of the Holy Spirit, the victory constitutes a judgment of Christ upon the particular sin.

The members of the Body of Christ are to walk in absolute righteousness and holiness of deed, word, motive, and imagination. God's judgment is upon His own household in these days. God can have no fellowship with the evil works of darkness, and neither can His children. We must learn to put to death the deeds of the flesh through the wisdom and power which the Holy Spirit provides.

The second area of redemption, that of sanctification, is a protracted, actual death of the compulsion to sin which resides in our flesh. It is a protracted, spiritual resurrection as we change over from walking in the sins of the flesh to walking in the holiness of the Life of the Holy Spirit. The "dying" consists of a long series of lessons in learning how to live, walk, speak, think, fight, and minister in the Spirit of God.

Such total sanctification of behavior requires a period of time for its accomplishment, and sometimes we become discouraged "in the wilderness." But there does come an end to the instruction, at least for the present stage of our development. We will "graduate" eventually. So do not allow yourself to become weary in the battle. Your end will be glorious.

But we have so much to learn about the Person, purpose, will, and way of the almighty God of Heaven!

In the preceding paragraphs we have discussed the *sanctification* phase of Christianity. Every person who would be in the Body of Christ must appear here. We must be baptized in the

Holy Spirit. Upon entering into the Life of the Spirit we begin to receive power to minister, and also power to bear the fruit of the image of the moral character of Christ (Galatians 5:22, 23).

The law of the Spirit of Life guides us in the putting to death of the deeds of our body. We must confess our sins, as the Spirit directs. We must submit ourselves to God, draw near to God, and resist the devil.

CONQUEST: THE THIRD AREA OF REDEMPTION

Salvation from Divine wrath is the first area of redemption. Salvation includes leaving the spirit of the world, and also the birth of Christ in us.

Sanctification is the second area of redemption. Sanctification has to do with learning to follow the wisdom, energy and enablement of the Holy Spirit rather than the wisdom, energy and enablement of the natural man. The natural man is the human, soulish, flesh and blood personality which was born of our human parents. Contained within our natural personality is a strong tendency toward sin, pride, and rebellion against God.

Conquest is the third area of redemption. Conquest is the level at which we gain victory over the spirit of the world; victory over our carnal lusts; victory over Satan; victory over our own pride and self-seeking. These victories are begun as soon as we are saved, but they grow into their fullest development as we are willing to follow Christ into perfect obedience to God.

Total victory is made possible through the blood of the Lamb; through the testimony which the Holy Spirit works in us; and through our willingness to love not our own life unto the death (Revelation 12:11).

Initial salvation, the first area of redemption, makes it possible for us to enter into the plan of redemption. Sanctification, the second area, is a school. It is the place where we make the transition from the life of the flesh to the life of the Spirit.

Conquest, the third area, is the end product, the goal, of the first two areas. In the realm of conquest we enjoy the fruitfulness and dominion promised to the heirs of the Kingdom of God.

The precious blood of Jesus leads the way toward conquest. The Holy Spirit testifies to us, in us, and through us, moving us along toward the rest of God—that place of perfect victory in Christ.

Final victory depends upon our willingness to allow God to slay our will. We must be willing to deny the *self*. Death to our own will is the deepest of the deaths that we die, and it leads to the fullness of resurrection glory.

In initial salvation we are assigned to the death of Christ and we share with Him in His resurrection.

In sanctification we die to the desires of our flesh and mind and we are raised up into the Life of the Holy Spirit.

In conquest we die to our deepest level of *self*—the origin and source of ego and identity. God has His own ways of getting at that center of our being, often using suffering as a tool.

If we allow the Lord to enter the source of our individuality we will be raised up into the fullness of fruitfulness and dominion in God the Father as one of His eternal servants (Revelation 22:3; Philippians 2:5-9).

It is true of all living creatures, whether physical or spiritual, that they have wills of their own. Mules, men, and angels all have wills of their own.

In bringing us to the fullness of conquest God does not take away or destroy our will. Rather, God transforms our will until our will corresponds to His will.

It is very difficult to die to the deepest levels of the will, even for the most devout Christian. We are glad to be saved from wrath and to be accepted of the Father. We are thankful to be rid of the sins of the flesh and the other bondages which Satan places upon us.

But the re-creation of our will, the death to that which in many instances is lawful, is not easy to accept. However, death to self-will leads to the highest realms of responsibility and service in God.

35 For whosoever will save his life shall lose it; but whosoever shall lose his life for my sake and the gospel's, the same shall save it.

—Mark 8

But it is not easy or pleasant to lose one's life!

There are many flaws in the human will. These flaws must be corrected by the grace of God working through the Lord Jesus Christ before we can serve as a king, priest, and prophet in the very Presence of the Lord God of Heaven.

Some of the flaws are as follows: presumption, personal ambition, disobedience, double-mindedness, suggestibility, man-pleasing, self-aggrandizement, stubbornness, pride, self-pity, self-destruction, self-preservation. Jesus Christ was probed for these flaws during His three temptations (Luke, Chapter 4). Christ passed the tests with honors!

> **13 Keep back your servant also from presumptuous *sins;* let them not have dominion over me: then shall I be upright, and I shall be innocent from the great transgression.**
>
> **—Psalms 19**

We Christians are to walk in the way that Christ directs us and not attempt to force spiritual results before the Lord prepares the time and place. There is a great difference between presumption and aggressive faith, although sometimes we have to be very prayerful in order to distinguish between the two. Presumption leads to sin and defeat. Faith leads to victory.

No person can serve the Lord and personal ambition at the same time. He will end up hating one and cleaving to the other.

Perhaps some of the principal motives behind the desire of the Jewish elders to crucify the innocent Christ were their envy, personal ambition, pride of station, desire for self-aggrandizement, and instinct for self-preservation. They were fearful that Christ was threatening their position as the leaders of Israel.

An uncrucified will can lead to very great tragedy in the household of God!

Jonah was a *disobedient* prophet. The nation of Israel, from the time that the people demanded a king until the carrying away into Babylon, witnessed few periods in its history when God was able to bless the nation because of obedience to His ways.

It requires the resources of Heaven and earth in order for the Holy Spirit to create obedience to the Lord in the will of a human being. We are by nature deeply and essentially disobedient to the will of God. We have to *learn* obedience, and it is a difficult curriculum.

A double-minded person is unstable in all of his ways and can get nowhere at all with God because he cannot make up his mind. Double-mindedness is a flaw in the will.

The Christian who is suggestible is unable to proceed straight on in God's will because he is open to all voices. Do you recall the prophet who was led into disobedience by the suggestion of an older prophet? (I Kings, Chapter 13).

It is well that we "salute no man by the way," so to speak, but steadfastly go about our business in the Lord without being led astray by the suggestions of others. We are not recommending that we refuse to heed the advice and counsel of other Christians, because it is a fact that there is wisdom in the multitude of counselors. Rather, we are speaking of being led off course by suggestions and not bringing each decision that we make into careful prayer before the Lord.

It is impossible to be a prophet if we are given to man-pleasing. Jesus never went out of His way to "sell" the Gospel or to please His listeners. "The fear of man brings a snare." If we fear the "faces of clay" before us we will never be free to declare the whole counsel of God. We must prepare the Divine food and make it palatable so that the sheep will be inclined to eat. But we are never to hold back from that which the Holy Spirit is speaking in order that we may gain the approval and support of our audience.

Self-pity or over-harsh criticism of ourselves is not pleasing to the Lord and has no place in the Kingdom of God.

It is impossible for us to be God's prophet, priest, and king, God's servant, in other words, while we are subject to presumption, or personal ambition, or disobedience, or double-mindedness, or suggestibility, or man-pleasing. Christ is able to correct these flaws in the will so that the will begins to correspond to the will of God.

THREE DEATHS AND THREE RESURRECTIONS

In the first death and resurrection, that of salvation, we pass from spiritual death unto spiritual life in the Presence of God.

In the second death and resurrection, that of sanctification, we pass from sinful behavior to holy behavior—behavior which is free from the lusts of the flesh.

In the third death and resurrection, that of conquest, we pass from self-will to God's will; from self-centeredness to God-centeredness; from self-love to the love of God; from self-seeking to the serving of the Lord Jesus Christ.

As soon as we possess complete and perfect spiritual life in body, soul, and spirit; complete and perfect liberty in body, soul, and spirit; and complete and perfect Divine will in body, soul, and spirit, having been joined perfectly to God through Christ; then we have been fully redeemed. Then we are able to receive the fullness of the abiding of the Father and the Son through the Holy Spirit.

The end product of all three deaths and resurrections is our acceptance by the Lord God and our rest in Him. In the third death and resurrection we die to the imperfections of our will and are raised up into the Presence and fellowship of the Father. It is a reaping unto the Father. It includes the crucifixion of our will.

The means to the righteousness of the first resurrection is the blood of Jesus Christ. We overcome through means of the precious blood of the Lamb of God.

The means to the liberty of the second resurrection is the Holy Spirit. The Holy Spirit brings us into perfect accord with the written Word of God. We overcome sin through means of the wisdom and power given to us by the Holy Spirit.

The means to the fruitfulness and dominion of the third resurrection is the interaction of the power of Christ's resurrection and the fellowship of His sufferings. We overcome self-will by loving not our lives unto the death. This is the path to the throne of Christ.

It may be true that each area of redemption has its counterpart in the heavenlies. We live spiritually in the heavenlies and naturally upon the earth at the same time. The saved begin to experience the joy and peace of Heaven while they yet are upon the earth. Isn't that true!

The second realm of the heavenlies seems to be that of spiritual activity and battle. Many passages of the Scriptures give us insight into the turbulence and conflict of the second area (Job 1:6; Daniel 10:13; Revelation 12:7; for example).

The third realm of the heavenlies may be that of the throne of Almighty God and of the Lamb. Jesus Christ abides at this level, as do the most holy, glorious and mighty of the angelic creatures.

Every Christian has been raised spiritually in Jesus Christ to the right hand of God. Through the precious blood of his Redeemer he has access to the very throne of God, there to offer adoration and to make his needs known to the Father. But the extent to which the saint is able to *abide* in Christ in every situation depends upon his willingness to allow the grace of God to work redemption in him.

How blessed to be released from the bondage of having to have our own way! God strikes down our youthful glee, our striving for position and preeminence, our impulsive enthusiasms.

The third death requires a period of time for its accomplishment. It is a protracted death to our tendencies toward presumption, toward the desire to be pleasing to our hearers, to gain the admiration and support of people. It is a protracted resurrection into rulership with God and restful service to Him in our land of promise.

As soon as we have been saved from wrath, set free from the bondages of sin, and transformed from self-centeredness to Christ-centeredness, then we are ready for the making alive of our mortal body. This will occur instantaneously, for those who have made themselves ready, at the glorious appearing of our Lord and Savior, Jesus Christ.

The third death and resurrection is necessary for the fullness of the image, union, fruitfulness, and dominion which accompanies joint-heirship with Jesus Christ. It is a death to attempting to serve God in our own wisdom and power. It is a judgment upon us as individuals, that is, upon the deepest center of will and being.

The fullness of the inheritance will be assigned to those who are faithful to God at this level of redemption.

The third death is typified by the crossing of the River Jordan. It is a change from Moses, the shepherd, to Joshua, the commander of battle. It is the throne phase of Christianity.

The third death and resurrection bring us into the rest of God, into the image of Christ, into the realm of power, into the consummation of redemption. The servant of the Lord must be in the image of Christ, of the Divine Substance of Christ, of the Divine Nature of Christ.

The composite Servant of the Lord is Messiah–Head and Body (Isaiah, Chapters 42 and 43).

As soon as God has brought His sons through the three areas of redemption it will be time for the Lord Jesus to appear, the time of the revealing of the sons of God (Romans 8:19). The entrance of Jesus Christ and His brothers into the earth will cause Armageddon, the confrontation between Jesus Christ and Antichrist.

Prior to Armageddon, the sons of God must come to know Jesus Christ, the power of His resurrection, the fellowship of His sufferings. Then they will be ready to put down all opposition to the rule of Christ. Jesus Christ is King of kings and Lord of lords. The entire creation, whether of the heavens, the earth, or the realms beneath the earth's surface, must bow the knee to Him.

Are you willing to have the "sentence of death" in yourself, and not trust in yourself but in God Who raises the dead? Are you willing to be troubled on every side, perplexed, persecuted, cast down, as you attempt to follow the Lord? Are you ready to say "Yes" to the death of the "I will"?

If you consent to die the death that God requires of you as an individual you will cross over Jordan, so to speak, and begin to conquer your land of promise. You will enter into the Holy of Holies and abide there. You soon will be eating of the "old corn of the land" with the Lord Jesus. You shall fully know and understand as you are fully known and understood.

We have termed the third area of redemption the *conquest* phase of Christianity. Every believer who would rule with Christ must move on into this realm. We must accept the power of His resurrection, and that power will be wrought in us as we are willing to share in His sufferings. This is the route to becoming a part of the Servant of the Lord, and to fighting alongside the Lord in His war against His enemies.

We must accept the sentence of death and learn to trust in God Who raises the dead. We must never attempt to serve God out of ambition or presumption, or neglect to serve Him because of fear, double-mindedness, or disobedience. Experience teaches us to serve from our position on the cross, and to bear our own cross after Jesus. The cross works a perfect work in us. The cross is the wisdom of God!

Until a Christian consents to serve Christ after this fashion he may be alive unto God, and he may have the victory over many of the sins of the flesh, but he still is in bondage to his own will. He is to allow Christ to bring him over Jordan until he can testify: "I am crucified with Christ; nevertheless I live; yet not I, but Christ liveth in me" (Galatians 2:20).

The material creation is waiting in the chains of corruption and futility until God's sons have been brought through the death of their wills; until King Jesus rather than King Self is sitting upon the throne of their personalities (Romans 8:19–21).

Death to self is the third area of redemption. From this vantage point the sons of God will be revealed.

Redemption includes the establishing of a relationship with God such that perfect freedom from the guilt, bondage, and effects of sin is obtained, and also release from the bondage of self-will.

The person who is wise, whether he or she may be young or old, will turn away from everything else in life, if need be, in order to more perfectly lay hold upon the fullness of redemption. It is the Father's good pleasure to bring many sons through every aspect of redemption all the way to the full measure of the glory of God.

There is no route to complete and perfect redemption other than through means of battle against the adversary. Satan is our enemy, and he will use any and every device to block our attempts to escape from his influence. But Jesus Christ is greater than Satan!

One of God's greatest pleasures arises from beholding one of His sons or daughters lay hold upon the grace and virtue which God has provided through Christ, escaping thereby from every unclean influence. God anoints us with the Holy Spirit when we love righteousness and hate iniquity, and when we are perfectly obedient to Him.

Christ asks you: "Will you be saved?"

If your answer is "Yes," He will bring you through death and resurrection.

Christ asks you: "Will you follow the Holy Spirit in sanctification?"

If your answer is "Yes," He will bring you a second time through death and resurrection.

Christ asks you: "Will you lose your life for My sake and the Gospel's?"

If your answer is "Yes," He will bring you a third time through death and resurrection.

What are your answers to His three questions?

3

Conquest—The Third Area of Redemption

There are other titles which we could have assigned to the third area of redemption, such as *consecration*, or *perfection*, or *throne-life*. But the term *conquest* suggests the warfare which is necessary for entrance into the promised-land rest of God; and also suggests victory in Christ—the positive, dynamic, faith-filled Christian discipleship which keeps on marching toward the "city which hath foundations."

We are always to be pressing on toward the fullness of Christ in God.

DEFINITION OF CONQUEST

1 I BESEECH you therefore, brethren, by the mercies of God, that ye present your bodies a living sacrifice, holy, acceptable unto God, *which is* your reasonable service.

2 And be not conformed to this world: but be ye transformed by the renewing of your mind, that ye may prove what *is* that good, and acceptable, and perfect, will of God.

—Romans 12

It is the will of God that Christians not only be saved and sanctified, but that they fight on to total reconciliation with God.

Being saved means that we have been absolved of guilt and will be carried right on through to the new Heaven and earth reign of Christ.

Being sanctified means that we are now following the Holy Spirit in the diligent application of our gifts and ministries, and also in the putting to death of the deeds of the flesh.

Being conquerors means that we attain to the fullness of fruitfulness and dominion. Laying hold upon the inheritance to this extent requires that we choose to love not our life unto the death. We are willing to suffer delayed gratification of our most fervent desires. In some instances the delay may be of several years' duration.

We are ready to deny our own desires, our own lives—all of that to which we have a "right." It is the place of unquestioned obedience as a soldier of Christ, as a servant of the Lord.

Not only are we willing to suffer delayed gratification—for years if so desired by the Lord—but we are also willing to continue doing things for which we have no heart, in which we take no delight.

We do what the Lord tells us to do, and we do it without complaining and without blaming others. As far as it is possible for us to do so, we rejoice in the Lord and look for blessings in the difficult circumstances. Total reconciliation to God, the fullness of victory in Christ, requires that we give our best to the Master without grumbling and complaining.

Walking in the sins of the flesh brings misery and death. Righteousness works peace in us and causes us to be fruitful and content in this life, even though we always will have tribulation on earth before Jesus appears (John 16:33; Acts 14:22; Revelation 1:9).

The realm of conquest is a deepening and broadening of the process of sanctification. In order for us to achieve total victory in Christ, all of that which we are, do, and possess must be brought through the Divine fire.

Conquest requires a pruning back of our "rightful" status, accomplishments, and possessions. The Spirit of God beckons us toward the place of denial, of crucifixion, of the loss of life. Such loss is not easy to accept, but it is the only path to union with God and fruitfulness and strength in the Kingdom of God.

Referring back to Romans 12:1, 2 we find that it is the *body* which is to be offered. This is the daily offering of our fleshly nature, and it requires considerable strength of spirit on our part in order to hold up our beastly self-life until God consumes the sacrifice.

> **1 ". . . that ye present your bodies a living sacrifice, . . ."**
>
> **—Romans 12**

Presenting our bodies a living sacrifice is no easy task. What is being set forth here is that in each day of life on earth we are to seek the mind of Christ as to what is important for the day. Our body is our link with the earth and with the world.

When God requires the sacrifice of our body He is asking for the entire course of our existence on the earth. Daily life on earth has to do with the desires and problems of the body. If we stop to think about it, the conduct of affairs on earth has to do almost exclusively with that which is happening to, with, and in our body. Except for a comparatively small amount of religious effort which attempts to cultivate the spirit, the whole of life is centered upon the enjoyment of the soul through the body.

> **19 "And I will say to my soul, Soul, thou hast much goods laid up for many years; take thine ease, eat, drink, *and* be merry."**
>
> **—Luke 12**

The soul satisfies itself through the body in eating, in drinking, and in being merry. But God calls for the daily sacrifice of the body and of the corresponding soulish desires.

Notice that we are to present our bodies as a "living" sacrifice. It would be so much easier if we could offer a "dead" sacrifice, "go into neutral" and resign ourselves to a "don't care" attitude of mental passivity. If we could flee to a place of hiding and spend our days in contemplation it might be easier.

But to stay alive in God with all of our powers alert and our will sharp and decisive, full of energy, ambitions, desires of all kinds, but always allowing God to blunt our thrusts as He will—that requires considerable determination.

The presenting of the body as a living sacrifice, holy, acceptable unto God, is a Christian act of worship. Instead of offering a young bull, a sheep, a goat, or a bird, we offer our bodies as a whole ascending (burnt) offering to the Lord. And we do it every day!

> **2 Speak unto the children of Israel, and say unto them, If any man of you bring an offering unto the LORD, ye shall bring your offering of the cattle, *even* of the herd, and of the flock.**
>
> **—Leviticus 1**

The first chapter of Leviticus describes the burnt (ascending) offering. Of the five principal offerings, the Altar was named after the burnt offering. It was referred to as the Altar of Burnt Offering. It can be seen that the *burnt* offering was of great importance in the sight of God.

The burnt offering was not a sin offering but an offering of devotion and consecration.

> **3 If his offering *be* a burnt sacrifice of the herd, let him offer a male without blemish: he shall offer it of his own voluntary will at the door of the tabernacle of the congregation before the LORD.**
>
> **—Leviticus 1**

We offer our consecration of our "own voluntary will." We choose to give all to Christ. He invites us but does not force us. We offer ourselves at the "door," that is to say, at the cross of Christ. All offerings are made at the cross. We take up our cross and follow Him. The cross of Christ is the only acceptable place of sacrificial death.

Devotees of other religions suffer pain and humiliation of the flesh, but their offering is of no value before the throne of God. The only acceptable place for the offering unto God is "at the door of the tabernacle of the congregation before the Lord."

We are not allowed even to choose our own death! We have to die the death that the Lord requires of us as individuals. Our dying must be the dying of the Lord Jesus as expressed in our unique personalities. We must be showing forth His death upon the cross, not our own religious zeal. Otherwise, it is of no profit before the Lord.

> **9 . . . and the priest shall burn all on the altar, *to be* a burnt sacrifice, an offering made by fire, of a sweet savour unto the LORD.**
>
> **—Leviticus 1**

The sacrifices of the Lord involve fire. When we determine that we are going to present a living sacrifice, then we have to set out the sacrifice and wait for the fire of God to consume the offering.

We cannot hurry God. Working with God requires great patience. God is never late. He is painstaking and thorough. Our problem is to keep the "birds of the air" off our sacrifice until God "passes between the pieces" (Genesis 15:10–17).

God requires of you and me that we present our bodies as a living sacrifice. He insists that we do so without delay. The time is short and we must set out our offering right now. Tomorrow Christ may be here, and we may have lost for eternity our one opportunity to take up our cross of self-denial and follow that social Outcast, Jesus Christ.

> **2 And be not conformed to this world: but be ye transformed by the renewing of your mind, that ye may prove what *is* that good, and acceptable, and perfect, will of God.**
>
> **—Romans 12**

The only possible way by which we can be transformed into Christ's image, escaping the molding influence of the spirit of the world, is to offer ourselves each day as living sacrifices. The only possible way by which we can prove the will of God for our life is by presenting our bodies each day as living sacrifices unto the Lord Jesus Christ, just as He presented His body each day as a living sacrifice unto the Father.

> **23 And he said to *them* all, "If any man will come after me, let him deny himself, and take up his cross daily, and follow me.**
> **24 "For whosoever will save his life shall lose it: but whosoever will lose his life for my sake, the same shall save it. . . ."**
>
> **—Luke 9**

Notice the free choice: "If any man will come after me"! It is up to us as individuals. But if we choose to come after Him, then we have to deny ourselves, setting aside our own interests in favor of the interests of Christ until our lives upon the earth have been terminated.

The setting aside of life must be performed consciously, conscientiously, and consistently on a daily basis. We must take up our cross of self-denial and follow Christ every day of our pilgrimage upon the earth.

There is nothing to be gained by refusing to give over life to Christ. But the cost of refusing is exceedingly great! There is so very much to lose!

If we seek to save ourselves from the death to self which Christ requires we end up losing life. But if we give over life for His sake, the Divine promise is that we will save our lives. We save our lives in Christ and we are resurrected into glory, having emerged unscathed from the fire of sacrifice and judgment.

Our part is to tell God that we wish to take up our cross and follow Christ. God's part is to take us at our word and to furnish the appropriate circumstances. This He does–thoroughly, ingeniously, effectively.

> **8 *We are* troubled on every side, yet not distressed; *we are* perplexed, but not in despair;**
> **9 Persecuted, but not forsaken; cast down, but not destroyed;**
> **10 Always bearing about in the body the dying of the Lord Jesus, that the life also of Jesus might be made manifest in our body.**
> **–II Corinthians 4**

There are several benefits which result from our being willing to accept the death which God sends our way. Two of them are as follows: (1) fruitfulness in the impartation of the glory of Christ to other people; and (2) the receiving of God's eternal strength which enables us to take dominion in the contest at hand.

God brings His strength through means of our weakness. The almighty authority and power of our Lord Jesus Christ flows forth from His crucifixion.

> **15 For all things *are* for your sakes, that the abundant grace might through the thanksgiving of many redound to the glory of God.**
> **16 For which cause we faint not; but though our outward man perish, yet the inward *man* is renewed day by day.**
> **–II Corinthians 4**

The perishing of Paul's outward man, as he gave his life over to the will of the Lord Jesus, resulted in the Life of Jesus being made manifest in Paul's physical body. The resurrection Life of Christ which thus was manifested, brought the glory of God to the listeners, and has brought that same glory to those who have read Paul's epistles throughout the centuries of the Christian era.

Divine Life was made available to people as the Apostle Paul was willing to lay down his life. God's Life must flow from someone's death—*death* meaning the giving over of life and activities to the Lord.

When Paul witnessed the Divine Life which was being revealed to others, then he was able to keep from fainting. Our determination to obey Christ is strengthened when we can see other people begin to partake of the Divine Glory.

Paul speaks further of the second benefit—that of the receiving of God's eternal strength such that we are able to gain dominion over those forces which would resist the doing of God's will.

> **17 For our light affliction, which is but for a moment, worketh for us a far more exceeding *and* eternal weight of glory;**
>
> **—II Corinthians 4**

The "weight" of glory referred to here is Paul's house from Heaven, mentioned in Chapter 5 of II Corinthians. Paul's house is a vehicle of unimaginable power and authority—an eternal, incorruptible source to him of liberty in God, of breadth of service, of glory, of joy, of life. When we respond properly to the afflictions of our death in Christ, weight is added to the house which will descend upon us from Heaven at the time of the first resurrection from the dead.

Our willingness to abide with Christ in the furnace of testing causes a Divine purity and an overcoming strength to be developed in us. The Divine Gold in our being is purified and the "bronze" in our personality which results from the judgment of God that works in us becomes pure and glowing.

Marvelous things happen to us in the furnace of tribulation, not the least of which are the companionship of the Son of God, and the burning away of our bonds.

Both fruitfulness and dominion result from our death in Christ.

> **24 "Verily, verily, I say unto you, Except a corn of wheat fall into the ground and die, it abideth alone: but if it die, it bringeth forth much fruit. . . ."**
>
> **—John 12**

It is God's way that we bear fruit through means of our death. There are many Scriptural examples of this principle of life out of death. The greatest example is that of the Lord Jesus Christ. Christ performed many miracles and taught truth as no other man before or since has taught it.

But it is from His death that the salvation of mankind has come!

Paul the apostle ministered to people in what is now southern Europe. Perhaps several thousand people heard Paul teach and preach during his lifetime, and witnessed the miracles which God wrought by his hands.

But Paul's knowledge of Christ which he recorded in his letters to the young churches has produced eternal life in millions upon unnumbered millions of souls. That knowledge of Christ resulted from Paul's willingness to "fill up that which is behind of the afflictions of Christ in my flesh for his body's sake, which is the church" (Colossians 1:24).

The sufferings associated with our consecration sometimes have to do with the bringing of life to other people.

If we insist upon serving Christ on our own terms, having our own way, refusing to deny ourselves at His request, then we may pursue "Christian work" but we will "abide alone." We can only bring forth the fruit of Christ through means of death in Christ.

Judge Samson is a type of the Church in the last days. His hair represents his consecration. His enormous strength was related directly to his uncut hair.

Samson enjoyed the pleasures of this world until the world uncovered the secret of his strength. We marvel at the willingness of Samson to cast away his great gift from God. But we throw away our spiritual strength when we become involved with the world, the flesh, and the devil.

The Church possessed enormous spiritual strength in the first century. But because of the willingness of subsequent leaders to socialize with the world, and to adopt human solutions to the problems of the Church, the consecration and separation of the Church from the world was impaired.

The inevitable occurred! The Church lost its spiritual

strength. Then the world was able to blind the Church to its ability to see Christ.

The world bound the Christian Church with the chains of God's judgment and put it to work "grinding away in prison," attempting to please a world system which always rejects the Lordship of Christ (Judges 16:21).

Whenever a Christian loses his consecration, his separation unto the Person and will of Jesus Christ, his strength leaves him. He loses his vision of God and of Heaven. He becomes bound in affliction and trouble. He is "thrown into prison" and has to work for the world in order to preserve his existence.

But since the time of Martin Luther, the "hair" of the Church is beginning to grow back. The consecration and separation is returning. The world cannot see this occurring anymore than the Philistines were able to perceive the danger of Samson's hair growing back.

The day will come when the flood of filth will fill the earth and the demons of Hell will make the Christians come out from their prison of shame and weakness and "make sport" for them. We are entering into the days of complete deriding and despising of the Christian churches by the peoples of the earth.

The blind Samson was led out by a lad and he played the clown for the entertainment of the Philistines. Very often today the churches are so pathetically eager for a wink of approval from the local community leaders that they will "play the clown" for the applause of the world, hoping to ingratiate themselves and win the approval of worldly people. This is done in the hope that those people will be "won for Christ."

But the Philistines in their ignorance (and the wicked always fall into their own traps!) placed the long-haired Hebrew between the two supporting pillars of the temple of Dagon. Evil spirits and evil people always end up bringing to pass the will of God and heaping destruction upon themselves.

Samson called out to God and asked to be avenged for the loss of his two eyes. In the last days before Jesus appears, the consecration of the Church will be renewed and the Christians will cry out to God because of the darkness and oppression which has come upon the Church and the earth through the rulership of the forces of Hell.

At that time the two hands of the Church will be guided (by a "lad"?) to the supporting pillars of the kingdom of darkness. The Church will place its right hand of the power of the Holy Spirit upon one pillar and its left hand of the blood of the Lamb upon the other pillar.

Then the Church will bow itself before God's throne with all of its might in the fullness of the death of total consecration to God's will. The result will be that the entire kingdom of darkness will come crashing down to utter destruction. Satan will be crushed under the feet of the Church. The Seed of the Woman (Christ in the saints) will tread Satan's head underfoot.

The Church by its death to self-will and self-seeking will bring forth greater liberation to the people of the world in the last days than it has been able to do through its own efforts during the two thousand years of its history.

At the time of greatest darkness upon the earth the saints will attain a level of consecration deeper than has ever been true before—deeper than that of the believers of the first-century churches (with the exception of the apostles and other notable men and women of God). The result will be a move of God through the Body of Christ which will destroy the entire kingdom of Satan.

> **30 . . . So the dead which he slew at his death were more than *they* which he slew in his life.**
>
> **—Judges 16**

Fruitfulness and strength result from our death in Christ.

Consider Abraham! Beyond all doubt, the high point in Abraham's life was the offering up of Isaac and the restoration of Isaac to him. Death and life go together. Those who are willing to go through God's assigned deaths will come to know the power and glory of God's resurrections.

There are some aspects of redemption which come about through the death of Christ and some aspects which come about through His resurrection. We cannot obtain the desired goal of rest in God through death alone or through resurrection alone.

We must have both death and resurrection in order to achieve the will of God.

So great was the pleasure of God over the obedience and faith of Abraham that God called to him out of Heaven. There are not many instances recorded in the Scriptures in which God spoke to people from Heaven. This was a very special occasion.

Abrahma here typifies the saint who is brought to the limits of consecration and faithful obedience to God. When we consider all that was involved in this incident we are staggered at the degree of consecration which God required and also at the strength of obedience residing in Abraham, he being more than one hundred years of age at the time.

We appreciate this quality of stern obedience in the Lord Jesus. But Jesus is so much better than we that we are not too astonished at His willingness to go to death, even though His death was so much more painful spiritually and physically than anything we can imagine.

Abraham, however, was a human as frail as any of us. His performance in being willing to slay Isaac portrays the sublime heights which can be attained if we are faithful in pursuing Christ with all of our might.

Out of Abraham's consecration to the will of God came forth an exceedingly great amount of fruitfulness and an exceedingly great degree of strength and dominion.

> **17 That in blessing, I will bless thee, and in multiplying I will multiply thy seed as the stars of the heaven, and as the sand which *is* upon the sea shore; and thy seed shall possess the gate of his enemies;**
>
> **—Genesis 22**

The blessing which comes to us from reading of the life of Joseph is derived largely from the knowledge of the years which Joseph spent in prison, that is, of the days of his consecration and death to his own ambitions and desires.

Jonah, also, speaks to us of the life which comes forth out of death (Jonah 2:6).

One of the most dramatic and helpful examples of death in God is that of Job. Billions of people have lived upon our planet. Job was one person from among those multitudes. Yet, few people have made an impact upon the personalities of their fellow humans equal to that of Job. His name is a household word, at least among Christians. Why is that?

Job was a very wealthy man. He was not distinguished as a prophet, priest, or king, merely as a wealthy individual. Job followed after righteousness and hated wickedness.

But the priceless legacy which Job has left us is the story of his sufferings in the Lord, the account of his death and resurrection in God. The life of Job would have had a very small effect upon the rest of us if he had lived out his life without incident, as a wealthy, righteous person.

Job became one of God's eternal witnesses because of his sufferings and his restoration. Powerful interventions of God in the life of an individual produce a powerful witness of the Person and way of God. It is such death and resurrection which creates change in other people.

Both Abraham and Job teach us that whatever we receive from God must be received twice. Until God removes our gifts the gifts possess us. But after God has taken them away in the fire of His judgment, and then has restored those gifts which are part of His plan for our life, our gifts no longer possess us. We worship them no longer.

Instead we, under God in Christ, are set free from the bondages which can result from relationships with other people, from circumstances, and from things. After we have been set free from the bondages in our relationships with people, in our circumstances, and in our things, and worship and adore God alone, then we are ready to receive Divine fruitfulness and dominion.

One of the most important of the Old Testament portrayals of death and resurrection in consecration unto God occurred in the life of Jacob. It is found in the thirty-second chapter of the Book of Genesis.

Jacob had been blessed of God. But much of Jacob's achievement in life had been forced through means of guile and cheating. Finally there came a day when he had to return and face the consequences of his actions, particularly his actions concerning his brother, Esau.

Isn't it true that we accomplish much through guile and cheating? But there always comes that day when God calls us to death and resurrection in Himself. If we successfully endure our contest with the Lord we emerge from the battle greatly enlarged in fruitfulness and strength.

Jacob sent his family across the Jabbok, a tributary of the Jordan River, into the land of Canaan. But Jacob himself remained alone. This is a type of our giving all over to God in preparation for our struggle unto death and life.

> **24 And Jacob was left alone; and there wrestled a man with him until the breaking of the day.**
>
> **—Genesis 32**

We can bring no one with us through our consecration wrestling. It is well if there is another person in whom we can confide and seek counsel and prayer. But there is only so much that others can share, only so far they can go with us. Essentially we wrestle alone in the night. The contest is between God and His saint.

We wrestle "until the breaking of the day." If we let go we lose the fight. If we stay in the contest long enough the morning light will break.

> **25 And when he saw that he prevailed not against him, he touched the hollow of his thigh; and the hollow of Jacob's thigh was out of joint, as he wrestled with him.**
>
> **—Genesis 32**

The thigh of man is in the area of the loins. The loins are the place of both fruitfulness and strength, the center of reproduction and physical stamina and exertion. We are always affected in the realm of fruitfulness and strength when we prevail with God Almighty.

> **26 And he said, Let me go, for the day breaketh. And he said, I will not let thee go, except thou bless me.**
>
> **—Genesis 32**

In spite of his guile, Jacob was a determined individual. God told him that the morning was at hand. But Jacob was seeking God's peace, seeking God's blessing, seeking deliverance out of the hand of Esau, seeking the favor and protection of the Lord.

Jacob prevailed with God, just as we can prevail once we make up our minds that we *must* have the favor of God.

> **28 And he said, Thy name shall be called no more Jacob, but Israel: for as a prince hast thou power with God and with men, and hast prevailed.**
>
> **—Genesis 32**

Jacob means supplanter, schemer, trickster. *Israel* means contender with God. The change of name indicates a change of personality. Prior to the struggle Jacob was in the habit of getting what he wanted by means of trickery and scheming. After the struggle he came to realize that the only way to obtain anything of value is to receive it fairly from God. That is the lesson we learn when we die in Christ and are raised up in consecration unto God.

> **29 And Jacob asked *him*, and said, Tell *me*, I pray thee, thy name. And he said, Wherefore *is* it *that* thou dost ask after my name? And he blessed him there.**
>
> **—Genesis 32**

As a result of the wrestling match, Jacob became more interested in God than he was in obtaining the answer to his prayer. The very same change of attitude occurs in us. In the course of our consecration-wrestling we come into such closeness to God that we become more interested in God Himself than we are in obtaining what we sought originally.

> **30 And Jacob called the name of the place Peniel: for I have seen God face to face, and my life is preserved.**
>
> **—Genesis 32**

No man can see God and live! How then did Jacob live after seeing God face to face?

The answer is, a part of Jacob died. He died and was raised again in God, just as we die and are raised again as the result of our consecration-wrestling. We come to the point of believing that all hope is gone; but somehow our life is preserved. Not only do we now have the answer to our prayer, but—best of all—we have come to know the Lord.

> **31 And as he passed over Penuel the sun rose upon him, and he halted upon his thigh.**
>
> **—Genesis 32**

Jacob now had a lame hip and he limped for the remainder of his life. He had been touched in the region of fruitfulness and strength. Now he was bound forever to God, having always to depend upon God for help and support.

We too learn to depend always upon God for help and support, as a result of our consecration death in God. No longer are we able to accomplish our goals through means of our own will, abilities, and schemings. From this point on we are weak and have to depend upon God for all victory. In the sight of God, this is the necessary condition if we are to be entrusted with increased fruitfulness and Divine strength.

The eternal life we seek comes out of death. Aaron's rod sprouted with life after being laid up in the Holy of Holies. If we will place all of our ambitions and hopes before the Presence of the holy Fire, and then leave them there until the Lord moves, there will come forth the buds, blossoms, and almonds of eternal, incorruptible resurrection life.

The buds are the first sign of resurrection life. The blossoms are the forerunners of the fruit to come. The almonds are the end product—the Nature and Presence of Christ wrought within us.

Whatever comes forth after having been placed and left for a season in the Presence of the fire of God has been resurrected from the dead. It has been accepted eternally in the sight of God.

The only means by which the life of Christ can come to other people is through our deaths.

> **24 Who now rejoice in my sufferings for you, and fill up that which is behind of the afflictions of Christ in my flesh for his body's sake, which is the church:**
>
> **—Colossians 1**

Eternal life has come to the Body of Christ because Christ was obedient unto death. The resurrection life from God flows out of death just as crops on a farm come forth from the seed which has been cast into the ground.

The only way by which the life of Christ can keep on coming forth to the members of the Body of Christ is through the death of those who minister as they follow the Lord Jesus in denial of self.

People cannot live from that which we give to them out of our own personalities. People partake of God as the result of our having been willing to die the death which God has required of us. As we are willing to die to self, the life of God raises us up. In the process of that raising, the saints to whom we are ministering are nourished with the resurrection life which is raising us up.

> **20 I am crucified with Christ: nevertheless I live; yet not I, but Christ liveth in me: and the life which I now live in the flesh I live by the faith of the Son of God, who loved me, and gave himself for me.**
>
> **—Galatians 2**

If we are willing to be crucified with Christ, to enter into the sharing of His sufferings, we will deny ourselves to the point of death, as the Lord leads. We will set aside our lives each day and pursue His desires for us whether we enjoy them or not.

The result of such self-denial will be death to the first personality. But out of this death will flow His resurrection life. The result will be expanded areas of fruitfulness, plus the possession of the strength of God Himself. "Christ lives in me"! That is fruitfulness and that is Divine, eternal strength.

Are we willing to become servants of Christ, a part of the Millennial Servant of the Lord (Isaiah 42:1)? If so, we must walk humbly with God to the point of being deprived of our lawful rights. But the end will be a generation of fruit so great that it scarcely can be described. Notice the following:

> **33 In his humiliation his judgment was taken away: and who shall declare his generation? for his life is taken from the earth.**
>
> **—Acts 8**

Christ was deprived of the material blessings which were His right as a righteous son of Abraham. But who is able to measure the amount of fruit which has come to mankind as the result of the willingness of Christ to be thus deprived?

Philippians 3:10 speaks of our being brought into the fellowship of the sufferings of Christ and of our being made conformable unto His death. If we suffer with Christ through the depths of the consecration into which God leads us, then spiritual life is brought to other people.

Of course, we never suffer to *pay* for the sins of others. The payment was made once and for all by Christ Jesus. There is no more need for that. Rather, our suffering is the sowing of ourselves unto death in God. Then when the Spirit of God raises us from death, the power which raises us flows out toward other people and the result is life in them.

The sufferings of Christ into which we are brought are described in the fifty-third chapter of Isaiah. Again, let us state that we do *not* atone for the sins of others, as did the Lord Jesus Christ. Yet, we *are* called upon to suffer in God in order that the fruit and strength which flow from our ministry will be Divine and not merely human.

> **3 He is despised and rejected of men; a man of sorrows, and acquainted with grief: and we hid as it were *our* faces from him; he was despised, and we esteemed him not.**
>
> **—Isaiah 53**

The same type of rejection happened to Joseph, to Job, to Jeremiah, although not as severely as in the case of Jesus Christ. If we decide to take up our cross and follow Christ, then we very well may suffer despising, rejection, sorrow, and lack of esteem. And this from people whom we are attempting to serve!

> **7 He was oppressed, and he was afflicted, yet he opened not his mouth: he is brought as a lamb to the slaughter, and as a sheep before her shearers is dumb, so he openeth not his mouth.**
>
> **—Isaiah 53**

We may be called upon to suffer the envy of others, oppression, affliction, and yet be directed of the Lord to offer no complaint nor attempt to justify our position. It is not easy to travel the road of consecration with Christ Jesus; but it is the only route to the Presence and power of the Father.

God Almighty will accept only the life which He brings forth in us—life which flows out from the crucifying of our flesh and self-will. We are not to open our mouths, but allow God Himself to vindicate our behavior.

> **9 And he made his grave with the wicked, and with the rich in his death; because he had done no violence, neither *was any* deceit in his mouth.**
>
> **—Isaiah 53**

Jesus Christ set aside His own life unto the point of death. In this manner He overcame all the power of the enemy. It is difficult to imagine what Jesus must have felt when He heard Pilate in one breath declare Him to be perfectly innocent and in the next breath sentence Him to death as a criminal.

The injustice of it all! Pilate knew very well that only the envy of the leaders of Israel had brought Jesus of Nazareth to trial. If we will follow the Master we must be prepared to suffer this very type of perversity and unfair treatment.

In the eleventh verse we behold the fruit which resulted from the willingness of Christ to follow the Father through the death and resurrection of consecration. In the twelfth verse we see the strength and dominion which also have resulted from His obedience unto death.

> **11 He shall see of the travail of his soul, *and* shall be satisfied: by his knowledge shall my righteous servant justify many; for he shall bear their iniquities.**
>
> **—Isaiah 53**

Christ is going to witness the fruit of the travail of His soul. Much fruit has come forth already, throughout the two-thousand-year period since His crucifixion. But so great will be the increase of the fruit of Christ in the days to come that the entire earth will be filled with the Life and image of Christ.

Every saved person upon the earth will reveal something of the fruit of the travail of the soul of Christ when He endured the dark hour of Gethsemane.

We too will witness the travail of our souls. Although our portion is on a smaller scale than that of Christ, yet the principle remains the same. One day the Apostle Paul will be able to view the results of his faithfulness unto death. We believe that Paul will be satisfied when he is made aware of the incomprehensible extent of the effect of his epistles upon the history and civilization of the world.

We also, if we are called upon of God to endure severe pruning of our personalities and accomplishments, will experience a corresponding abundance of fruit.

The other product of our consecration unto death and resurrection in Christ will be greatly increased strength, responsibility, and opportunity for service.

> **12 Therefore will I divide him *a portion* with the great, and he shall divide the spoil with the strong; because he hath poured out his soul unto death: and he was numbered with the transgressors; and he bare the sin of many, and made intercession for the transgressors.**
>
> **—Isaiah 53**

Because Christ was willing to pour out his soul unto death He is going to receive the reward of the spoil due a conqueror. Strength to rule is the direct result of obedience to God. The only Christians who will attain the highest levels of rulership in Christ will be those of whom God requires the deepest depths of sufferings in Christ.

The crown flows out from the cross. If we suffer we will reign. If we enter the bond of His sufferings, then we will experience the power of His resurrection. It is the conqueror who is going to rule with Christ.

To sit on the right hand and the left hand of Christ is assigned to those so indicated by the Father. But of them will be required the drinking of the cup of Christ and a baptism of suffering like His.

There was no need for Christ to experience the first area of redemption, that of initial salvation, because He was guiltless in the sight of God.

There was no need for Christ to experience the second area of redemption, that of sanctification, because He was without inherited or acquired sinful tendencies and practices.

The only area of redemption of benefit to Christ Himself was that of self-denial. Christ learned obedience through the things which He suffered.

10 For it became him, for whom *are* all things, and by whom *are* all things, in bringing many sons unto glory, to make the captain of their salvation perfect through sufferings.

—Hebrews 2

8 Though he were a Son, yet learned he obedience by the things which he suffered;
9 And being made perfect, he became the author of eternal salvation unto all them that obey him;

—Hebrews 5

Jesus Christ was made perfect through suffering. Through suffering He learned obedience. We also are made perfect through suffering. Through suffering we learn obedience to God.

When Christ was in the flesh He offered up prayers and supplications with strong crying and tears unto Him Who was able to save Him from death (Hebrews 5:7). This reminds us of the wrestling of Jacob with the angel.

We also, as we become older and stronger in the Lord, find ourselves in the wrestling match with God. We grapple with God in the throes of death to our self-love. This is the area of conquest.

If we desire to go all the way through to the fullness of redemption, then we must die and be raised into the Person and Presence of the Father. Here is the ultimate in self-denial. Here is the ultimate in obedience. Here is the ultimate in fruitfulness. Here is the ultimate in Divine strength and dominion over the works of God's hands.

Once we have died this death and have been raised in this resurrection, the fire of God no longer can harm us. The second death has no more authority over us. We are alive in God eternally, having been declared to be a son of God by the resurrection from the dead. The sentence of the judgment upon us is that we be raised from the dead in the fullness of Divine Glory to meet the Conqueror as He descends from Heaven with His saints and holy angels.

The three areas of redemption accomplish many different goals, as far as we are concerned.

Salvation obtains for us preservation in the Day of Wrath.

Sanctification releases us from the bondages of our sinful flesh and carnal mind, so that we are free to pursue the Spirit-filled life of righteous and holy behavior, and of testimony and service in the will of God.

Conquest brings us into the fullness of our inheritance as sons of God.

The Book of Isaiah has a great deal to say about the Servant of the Lord.

> **1 BEHOLD my servant, whom I uphold; mine elect, *in whom* my soul delighteth; I have put my spirit upon him: he shall bring forth judgment to the Gentiles.**
>
> **–Isaiah 42**

Chapter 42, and other chapters of Isaiah, describe the ministry of Messiah–Head and Body. Christ (Messiah) is the Servant of the Lord God of Heaven. We are being created the fullness of this great Servant Who was, Who is, and Who is yet to come.

The Servant is the elect of God, just as Jesus said: "Ye have not chosen me, but I have chosen you, and ordained you, that ye should go and bring forth fruit" (John 15:16).

The Soul of God "delights" in His Servant. We are being created a delight to the Lord. "I have put my spirit upon him." The reason we have received the Holy Spirit is that we might become a part of God's Servant, God's Anointed Deliverer of whom the Hebrew prophets spoke.

"He shall bring forth judgment to the Gentiles." The ministry of the Servant, the Messiah, is that of judging and delivering the peoples of the earth, in addition to the establishing of Israel as God's people. The Servant of the Lord is going to proceed throughout the earth at the appearing of Jesus Christ, destroying sin and liberating the nations of the earth.

The entire kingdom of darkness will be crushed under the feet of the Servant of the Lord. No vestige of that kingdom will remain. All of the earth will abide under the law of Christ. The rod of iron will bring release to those who will obey Christ and receive His lordship. But the rod of iron will bring destruction to those who rebel.

> **2 He shall not cry, nor lift up, nor cause his voice to be heard in the street.**
>
> **—Isaiah 42**

The Servant of the Lord does not force people and circumstances in his own strength and scheming. He waits upon God until the Spirit of God brings all people, circumstances, and things into line with the will of God.

> **3 A bruised reed shall he not break, and the smoking flax shall he not quench: he shall bring forth judgment unto truth.**
>
> **—Isaiah 42**

God works patiently with each one of His elect until that individual learns to be patient. The Servant of the Lord learns from the Father to be gentle and to minister in patience and love. Many souls can be wrested from the fires of destruction if we do not lose our patience with them.

In the above verse (Isaiah 42:3) there is great hope for the weak Christian. It is our conviction that God is going to save the weak members of the Church and establish them in beauty and glory in the new Jerusalem.

> **4 He shall not fail nor be discouraged, till he have set judgment in the earth: and the isles shall wait for his law.**
>
> **—Isaiah 42**

As we die and are resurrected in God we come to many, many points of seeming failure, which tempt us with discouragement and disappointment. But then the touch of God strengthens us, and failure is transformed into victory. Encouragement comes forth from the grave of discouragement at the voice of Christ, and we receive that eternal strength and patience which are so very necessary to the accomplishment of the will of the Father.

> **19 Who *is* blind, but my servant? or deaf, as my messenger *that* I sent? who *is* blind as *he that is* perfect, and blind as the LORD'S servant?**
>
> **—Isaiah 42**

We have to die and be raised in God in order to attain that

perfect blindness and deafness. We find the same thought in II Corinthians 4:18.

> **18 While we look not at the things which are seen, but at the things which are not seen: for the things which are seen *are* temporal; but the things which are not seen *are* eternal.**

As we die in God we are sorely tempted to criticize other people and to attempt to place blame upon others for our troubles. Also, we become exceedingly vexed because of the wicked, unjust practices in the earth. Our faith is tried because what we see in the natural realm is so contrary to that which the Spirit of God is showing us to be the right way to live.

Our task–and it is very difficult at times–is to refuse to look at the things which are seen and to fasten our gaze upon Christ. This means that we must cease criticizing other people, cease blaming others for our problems, cease fretting over the wickednesses in the earth, and cease worrying over the possible outcomes of our impossible circumstances.

The Servant of the Lord is blind and deaf to the people, circumstances and things which are bringing him into the death and resurrection of perfect union with God. He waits patiently for the wisdom and power of the Father to relieve the pressure. God's Servant does not judge after the hearing of the ear or the seeing of the eye. He waits for the Word of the Lord before he passes judgment, or responds to a situation.

The resurrection power and life of God surrounds the Servant of the Lord.

> **2 When thou passest through the waters, I *will* be with thee; and through the rivers, they shall not overflow thee: when thou walkest through the fire, thou shalt not be burned; neither shall the flame kindle upon thee.**
>
> **–Isaiah 43**

Here is a portrayal of our conquest experience, our death and resurrection in the Father. We pass through the waters of trials, troubles, despairs, discouragements, humiliations, persecutions; and God is with us throughout each painful episode. We pass through the rivers of active oppositions, fightings, pressures, envyings; but they cannot possibly conquer us because of the resurrection life from the Father which keeps on protecting us, guiding us, and lifting us up.

We walk through the midst of God's judgment, but we become judgment-proof through means of the precious blood of Christ and through means of confessing and forsaking our sins. The flames roar up all about us but there is nothing left in us which will ignite.

We are becoming pure gold in God, and the heat and pressure no longer can harm us. The fiery trials only make us more pure. We are alive forevermore in Christ Jesus.

If we would become a member of the Servant of the Lord, of the Body of Messiah we must become "blind" and "deaf" to circumstances and people; to the means which God uses to bring us unto the death of ultimate obedience to Himself. The end result of such total obedience is extraordinary fruitfulness and irresistible might.

As to fruitbearing:

> **6 He shall cause them that come of Jacob to take root: Israel shall blossom and bud, and fill the face of the world with fruit.**
>
> **—Isaiah 27**

And as to overcoming strength:

> **14 Fear not, thou worm Jacob, *and* ye men of Israel; I will help thee, saith the LORD, and thy redeemer, the Holy One of Israel.**
>
> **15 Behold, I will make thee a new sharp threshing instrument having teeth: thou shalt thresh the mountains, and beat *them* small, and shalt make the hills as chaff.**
>
> **—Isaiah 41**

Mountains and hills symbolize the governments of the earth and the powers which rule in the earth. The Servant of the Lord is going to judge these governments, and bring them down into obedience to the Lord Jesus Christ. All opposition will be cut down into helpless chaff before the onslaught of the Servant of the Lord.

But such threshing and beating small is impossible until the Church is ready to become God's "worm." "Wormology" is one of the more important branches of theology. We may not enjoy the thought of becoming God's worm. We do not mind being termed a lion, or an eagle, or some other animal which commands respect. But a worm? Never!

It is impossible for the Christian Church to bring about the Kingdom of God in the earth other than by becoming a worm. Being a worm has nothing to do with compromising with the world or with currying favor with men. God's worms never attempt to build anything with the help or approval of the flesh. We do not need so much as a shoestring from the world. The less we lean upon the arm of flesh the better off we will be.

Being a worm means being meek in the sight of God. It means allowing our rights and privileges to be removed unjustly and not resorting to our own scheming and trickery in the attempt to bring about our own victories.

Being a worm means waiting upon God and allowing Him to deny us our desires and to bring us into unpleasant situations. The worm does not murmur, complain, or seek to justify its own position. The worm is God's worm, not man's worm. Our attitude and approach toward God must be one of humility and patience.

We are not to strike back as does a rattlesnake. We are to keep on burrowing through the messy problems and circumstances under which we are nearly suffocated. But in Christ we never suffocate because He raises us up continually.

For two thousand years the major segment of the Christian Church has attempted to accomplish the work of the Kingdom, and to impress the world with the rightness and power of its cause, through means of its own wisdom and strength. The Church desires to convince the world that the Church is of God and should be esteemed and its precepts obeyed.

But all such attempts are futile because the methods employed are contrary to the mind of God. In the last days, just before Christ appears, the Church will come to understand that God works through our death of perfect consecration and our obedience to Christ.

Our task is to allow God to have His way in us, to be perfectly obedient. Then, and only then, will the Holy One of Israel come thundering forth, bearing witness of Himself through the Body of Christ. When He does, and the Scripture promises that He will in the last days, the Body of Christ will be filled with glory and multitudes of earth's peoples will be brought into the righteous ways of the Lord.

In that hour of worm-like dependence, the Church, having wrestled with God unto the death, will hardly notice that all of its desires are being fulfilled in abundance. For now, as was true of Jacob, the eyes of God's saints will become so fixed upon God that everyone and everything else will fade away into secondary importance. The Church will become enraptured with the Person of Christ.

The single-minded, adoring contemplation of Christ will bring all other persons, circumstances, and things into proper perspective. Such gaining of perspective is true of each one of us today who is willing to trust God to the point of ceasing to press our own notions and allowing our worship of Him to ascend to first place in our faith and thoughts.

It may be true that the third area of redemption, that of self-denial, is the most trying and difficult of the three deaths and resurrections. But self-denial, the bearing of our personal cross, is the only route to the greatest fruitbearing and the greatest power and glory in Jesus Christ.

Are we willing to be brought to the point of ultimate obedience?

How does one come to the place of perfect obedience to the Father? First of all, we must give our consent to such total obedience and faithfulness to God. It is necessary that we tell the Lord Jesus with our mouth that we are determined, by the wisdom and strength which He provides, to follow Him with a perfect heart.

It is helpful to tell others of our determination. When the situation is appropriate, it is neither proud nor boastful to state that Jesus is our Lord and that by His grace we are going to serve Him with our whole life. A verbal statement of determination will help to strengthen resolve, and it will challenge others who may need that extra bit of encouragement to push them over the line of decision into the ranks of the conquerors in Christ.

Leading the life of victory in Christ does not require unusual will-power, spirituality, or any other extraordinary resource on our part. Every Christian should be and can be an overcomer in the Lord. Our part is to obey Christ when He commands us to do something. God's part is to make it possible for us to perform our act of obedience.

From our point of view, the concept that there is a permissive will of God for the disciple of Jesus is completely false. The only true disciple of Christ is the person who is following Jesus with singleness of purpose. The indecisive, half-hearted, guilt-ridden "profession" of Christ which we see about us is not Christian discipleship as described in the Scriptures!

There are many fine people who have come into our churches and who are upset about the sin in the earth. They may have received Christ as Savior and have been baptized in water. But until they receive Christ as their personal Lord they are not disciples of the Lord; they are not overcomers and the rewards assigned to the overcomers will not be given to them.

In some instances, the Christian believers have been deceived into assuming that the indecisive playing around the edges of the faith, the halfway measures of obedience, are acceptable to God the Father. Most assuredly they are not! God, in His great love, is waiting for us to climb up out of the valley of decision. Either we are obeying Christ or else we are not obeying Christ. There is no middle ground!

Each member of the Body of Christ must learn to bear endlessly with people who are attempting to come into a right relationship with God through Christ. We ought always to be full of encouragement, patience, understanding, toward the less fervent Christians.

But we will live to see the day when all of the wishy-washy, half-hearted temporizing is swept away by the broom of destruction. There will be no more halting between two opinions. In that Day there will be no person joined to the Body of Christ, to the Servant of the Lord, who has any reservations whatever about going through the full death and resurrection which God requires.

The Christian soldier carries his cross as a soldier. He marches after Christ. He is a son of God. He endures hardness.

His mind is girded with resolve to obey Christ through the sufferings which come his way. He renders immediate obedience as soon as he is certain that Christ indeed has spoken.

He wastes no time counting the cost. He is up and after Christ each day. He seeks the will of Christ with his whole heart. He is dependable, steady, faithful unto death.

In the areas of imperfection in his life he submits meekly to the rebukes and chastenings of his Lord. If you ask him if he is doing the will of Christ, he will answer, "Yes!" His conscience is clear. His heart does not condemn him.

If there is only one such person upon the earth, then there is only one disciple of the Lord Jesus Christ upon the earth. If there are ten such people upon the earth, then there are ten disciples of the Lord Jesus. In the present moment of history God is particularly interested in developing the quality of perfect obedience. In addition, many persons are being saved from wrath; still others are following on to increased knowledge of the redemption which is in Christ.

Will *you* be a soldier of Christ?

After we have given mental and vocal consent to being a servant of Christ, we must accept the joys and sorrows which will come to us. For the Father most certainly will take us at our word and will bring us successfully through the many experiences which are necessary for our perfecting in His Person and will.

Certainly, there is a price to pay for such glory. All precious commodities have a high cost.

But the cost of *not* following the Lord Jesus with a perfect heart is far, far greater than the cost of perfect obedience. The waters of eternal life are free. But the price of not obeying the Lord Jesus is our inheritance as a son of God. We ought to think twice before selling our inheritance as a son of God for the relationships, circumstances, and things of this world.

Do not lightly regard the fact that Jesus Christ, the King of glory, is offering to you the joy and blessing of the Fullness of His Presence!; His very throne!

The developing of obedience in us must run so deep that our mental and vocal consent is the merest beginning. The Spirit of God assumes the task of developing obedience in us. Then the hammering commences.

You see, we are being fashioned into the Mercy Seat–the place of reconciliation with God for all mankind. The Ark of the Covenant was overlaid with gold, representing the fact that our glorious house from Heaven is going to "swallow up" our mortal flesh (II Corinthians 5:4).

Also, our deepest inner being is becoming the gold of God's very Substance. We are being created the Mercy Seat, the Lid of Reconciliation, the place of the Presence of the Consuming Fire of Israel.

The Mercy Seat must be hammered into shape, it cannot be cast at once. Moment after moment, day after day, month after month, year after year, the hammering upon the Christ-filled personality continues. Will it never cease!

Each painstakingly-aimed hammer blow touches some nerve, some point of the old nature. The old passes away and the refined and shaped new takes its place. It is not a fun-filled game.

With endless patience God taps, taps, taps, taps. We are brought down to the border of discouragement. We come close to despair. God watches carefully for the breaking point, to see if we are getting too close to the edge of collapse.

> **15 For thus saith the high and lofty One that inhabiteth eternity, whose name *is* Holy; I dwell in the high and holy *place*, with him also *that is* of a contrite and humble spirit, to revive the spirit of the humble, and to revive the heart of the contrite ones.**
> **16 For I will not contend for ever, neither will I be always wroth: for the spirit should fail before me, and the souls *which* I have made.**
> **–Isaiah 57**

Day after day! Day after day! Is there no end to the hammering? But the Lord smiles patiently, having experienced those hammer blows Himself.

The will is ground in the mill of God, and the Substance of Christ is "beaten small" and pounded into the will until the two wills are indistinguishable. Each will is present, vital, undamaged, honed to razor sharpness. But the two wills, Christ's and ours, have been beaten fine and pounded together until God has been formed in us and is dwelling in us both to will and to do of His good pleasure.

Let us rejoice because the very Throne of Glory is being fashioned in us. Also, the defense of the Glory, the wall of the new Jerusalem, that eternal resistance against all sin, is being created within us (Isaiah 4:5).

Covering the Mercy Seat are the two cherubim of glory. One is wrath and the other is mercy. Wrath and mercy! The fullness of God's wrath and the fullness of God's mercy.

God does not sit upon the Mercy Seat. God dwells between the cherubim of glory. There is no need for God to sit anywhere for He is All-energy, All-power, All-authority, All-goodness, All-wrath, All-mercy. God is everywhere at once!

Christ is seated upon the highest Throne of Glory, and we are seated together with Him and in Him. However, in order to maintain our place in Him, to keep possession of our crown, we must allow the Father to bring us into perfect obedience, into the fullness of death and resurrection in Himself.

We are to follow the Holy Spirit in all matters. We cannot possibly take hold of the program of redemption and manage it. Each one of us has been called to a different place in God's Kingdom. Our death and resurrection in God will depend, as to its full extent, upon that place of responsibility and service to which we have been called. The calling of the Lord God of Heaven is upon us. Our task in life is to respond completely and wholeheartedly to that call.

The first and second deaths and resurrections are somewhat the same for everyone. We all must accept Christ and be saved; and we all are called upon to completely repudiate sin and to learn to live and walk in the Spirit of God.

But when we come to the area of conquest, while it most certainly is true that each one of us must say "Yes" to Jesus when He speaks to us, yet the outworking of death and resurrection in God varies from person to person.

There is only so much temptation we can stand! To aspire beyond our measure is to be plagued with spiritual ambition. Spiritual ambition runs uncomfortably close to Satan's rebellion. Let us be content, rather, with that which is required of us as an individual. The attendant challenges will prove to be as difficult as we are able to endure.

We have just set forth some of the aspects of the third platform of redemption, which we have termed *conquest.* We must cooperate with the Holy Spirit of God as He teaches us obedience through the things which we are suffering.

We are undergoing death to those elements of our personalities which are lawful and, from some points of view, apparently desirable. Enthusiasm and self-reliance are two examples. But these elements have never been resurrected in God. They are not part of Jesus Christ.

The death involved in conquest is in contrast to the first two deaths, death to the world and death to sin—death to those things which are undesirable and unlawful.

The area of conquest includes the total judgment upon all that the first personality is and does. It is the reaping unto the Father.

The three members of the holy Trinity have to do with all areas of redemption. But the Lord Jesus Christ is especially prominent in developing the area of salvation, because it is through His precious atoning blood that we are saved from wrath.

The Holy Spirit is especially prominent in developing the area of sanctification, because it is through the wisdom and power which the Holy Spirit provides that we are able to overcome the lust of the flesh, the lust of the eyes, and the pride of life.

The Father is especially prominent in the area of conquest. Even the Lord Jesus Himself had to undergo the perfecting of obedience to the Father.

All Christians know that God is the Father, that He is our Father. But we come to know the Father in an even greater measure when we allow the Holy Spirit to lead us into the fullness of death and resurrection in the realm of obedience to the will of the Father.

Christ asks you: "Will you lose your life for My sake and the Gospel's?" What is your answer?

Will you move past Pentecost on to Conquest?

4

The Blowing of the Trumpets

The heavy emphasis in the third area of redemption is upon our perfection, our obedience, our ascent to the throne of Christ, our fruitfulness, the dwelling of God in Christ in us, and the establishing of the Kingdom of God upon the earth.

The convocation of Trumpets occurred on the first day of the seventh month of the Jewish religious year. Today the observance is termed *Rosh Hashanah.* The blowing of the trumpet calls attention to the nearness of *Yom Kippur,* the Day of Atonement, which is celebrated on the tenth day of the seventh month.

The name of the seventh month of the Jewish sacred, ceremonial year is *Tishri. Tishri* is the seventh month of the ceremonial year but the first month of the agricultural year. Since the blowing of Trumpets is celebrated on the first day of the first month of the agricultural (civil) year, Trumpets (Rosh Hashanah) is New Year's Day of the civil year.

We see, then, that when we come to the three convocations of the third major Feast of Tabernacles, which are Trumpets, Day of Atonement, and the week of Tabernacles itself, we have come to the beginning of a new year in the Lord.

It is not that we forsake the previous lessons and ways through which the Lord has worked in and with us. Rather, it is that these previous experiences have brought us to the place of newness in Christ. We are becoming a completely new creation in Christ.

The Jews have two overlapping years, one beginning with the month of Passover *(Nisan),* the other year beginning with Trumpets *(Tishri).* So it is in the Kingdom of God. In our experience we have a "religious year" of faith, doctrines, and observances. They have to do with our "coming out of Egypt."

But when we come to Trumpets we are entering into the civil year of doing business for the Lord in the earth. *Trumpets* heralds the coming of the Kingdom of God into the earth.

First, the Lord of hosts enters into our hearts and sets up His throne there. After that, He is coming in the Kingdom-wide fulfillment of the blowing of Trumpets. The trumpet of the Lord shall sound, and the King, the Lord Jesus Christ, shall descend from Heaven with His saints and holy angels.

Every eye shall behold Him, and we, to the utter consternation, confusion, and terror of our enemies, shall be caught up in the clouds along with the dead in Christ to meet the Lord Jesus in the air. So shall we ever be with the Lord.

THE CONVOCATION OF TRUMPETS

The convocation of Trumpets which is the first of the three parts of the Feast of the Tabernacles, was the fifth of the seven Levitical convocations described in the twenty-third chapter of Leviticus.

> **24 Speak unto the children of Israel, saying, In the seventh month, in the first *day* of the month, shall ye have a sabbath, a memorial of blowing of trumpets, an holy convocation.**

The number *five* symbolizes the *beginning* of the Kingdom of God. You may recall that animal life was begun on the fifth day of creation. The bronze Altar of Burnt Offering (Exodus 27:1) was five cubits square. The height of the linen fence (Exodus 27:18) which surrounded the Tabernacle of the Congregation was five cubits.

Both the bronze Altar and the linen fence stood at places where an individual first encountered the Tabernacle of the Congregation. Five pillars supported the door of the Holy Place. The fifth article of furniture, the Altar of Incense, was placed directly before the Mercy Seat.

The blowing of Trumpets signifies the beginning of the conquest of the material creation by the Lord Jesus Christ working in and with His anointed Body.

Isn't it inspiring to realize that the greatest things in Christ are yet ahead of us?

Perhaps the most common reference to the trumpet in the Scriptures is in connection with warfare.

> 20 So the people shouted when *the priests* blew with the trumpets: and it came to pass, when the people heard the sound of the trumpet, and the people shouted with a great shout, that the wall fell down flat, so that the people went up into the city every man straight before him, and they took the city.
>
> —Joshua 6

> 20 And the three companies blew the trumpets, and brake the pitchers, and held the lamps in their left hands, and the trumpets in their right hands to blow *withal:* and they cried, The sword of the LORD, and of Gideon.
>
> —Judges 7

> 19 My bowels, my bowels! I am pained at my very heart; my heart maketh a noise in me; I cannot hold my peace, because thou hast heard, O my soul, the sound of the trumpet, the alarm of war.
>
> —Jeremiah 4

> 8 For if the trumpet give an uncertain sound, who shall prepare himself to the battle?
>
> —I Corinthians 14

The forces of righteousness and the forces of iniquity are drawing near to the battle of the ages. Although sin is to reach a hideous flowering in the earth, yet the end of darkness is at hand.

The Christian Church is in travail today, bringing forth the Body of Christ. As soon as Christ has attained the necessary level in His saints, then the battle will be joined. The kingdom of darkness will be cast out of the heavens first, and finally out of the earth.

The end is in sight! The full redemption of the Year of Jubilee is at hand! The wrestling match will be concluded when Christ in the Church pins the adversary to the mat once and for all.

Christ is passing among the members of His Body in these days, looking for those who will be faithful enough to be in His army. He requires officers and men of the sternest discipline. Will you be one of these?

The coming of Christ is the coming of the King, the Lord of Armies. His appearing is that of God's Conqueror Who is going to set up His reign in the earth. The trumpet of God will sound, announcing the Presence of the rightful King and Heir.

> **15 So David and all the house of Israel brought up the ark of the LORD with shouting, and with the sound of the trumpet.**
>
> **—II Samuel 6**

> **1 BLOW ye the trumpet in Zion, and sound an alarm in my holy mountain: let all the inhabitants of the land tremble: for the day of the LORD cometh, for *it is* nigh at hand.**
>
> **—Joel 2**

> **31 "And he shall send his angels with a great sound of a trumpet, and they shall gather together his elect from the four winds, from one end of heaven to the other. . . ."**
>
> **—Matthew 24**

> **52 In a moment, in the twinkling of an eye, at the last trump: for the trumpet shall sound, and the dead shall be raised incorruptible, and we shall be changed.**
>
> **—I Corinthians 15**

> **16 For the Lord himself shall descend from heaven with a shout, with the voice of the archangel, and with the trump of God: and the dead in Christ shall rise first:**
>
> **—I Thessalonians 4**

The trumpet of God announcing the return of the Lord Jesus is made up of seven trumpets.

> **2 And I saw the seven angels which stood before God; and to them were given seven trumpets.**
>
> **—Revelation 8**

The Lord shall appear and we shall be changed, at the sounding of the last of these trumpets.

> **15 And the seventh angel sounded; and there were great voices in heaven, saying, The kingdoms of this world are become *the kingdoms* of our Lord, and of his Christ; and he shall reign for ever and ever.**
>
> **—Revelation 11**

The convocation of Trumpets is celebrated by each of us as an individual as we welcome the Lord Jesus into our heart as King of kings and Lord of lords. The convocation of Trumpets will be celebrated in the Kingdom-wide fulfillment as He descends from Heaven to take over the rulership of the earth. This marks the establishing of the Kingdom of God upon the earth.

The eighth chapter of Revelation reveals the connection between Trumpets, which is the *fifth* Levitical feast, and the Altar of Incense, which is the *fifth* of the holy furnishings of the Tabernacle of the Congregation.

As the Spirit-empowered, Christ-filled prayer and praise ascends to the Father from the Body of Christ in the days in which we now live, the hand of God Almighty will be moved and He will command His angels to sound the trumpets announcing the return of the King.

> **2 And I saw the seven angels which stood before God; and to them were given seven trumpets.**
> **3 And another angel came and stood at the altar, having a golden censer; and there was given unto him much incense, that he should offer *it* with the prayers of all saints upon the golden altar which was before the throne.**
>
> **—Revelation 8**

The trumpet was employed to alert Israel and to prepare the nation for the march.

> **2 Make thee two trumpets of silver; of a whole piece shalt thou make them: that thou mayest use them for the calling of the assembly, and for the journeying of the camps.**
>
> **—Numbers 10**

Also, the trumpet was blown by the Church toward God, to remind Him of His Word concerning His chosen people.

> **9 And if ye go to war in your land against the enemy that oppresseth you, then ye shall blow an alarm with the trumpets; and ye shall be remembered before the LORD your God, and ye shall be saved from your enemies.**
>
> **—Numbers 10**

The trumpet represents the worship, supplication, and intercession which must proceed from the Church as it assembles to serve the Lord Jesus. We need to direct our attention toward Heaven, and not become too occupied with our horizontal needs and expressions. The first commandment is to love God with all of our heart, soul, mind, and strength.

> **10 Also in the day of your gladness, and in your solemn days, and in the beginnings of your months, ye shall blow with the trumpets over your burnt offerings, and over the sacrifices of your peace offerings; that they may be to you for a memorial before your God: I *am* the LORD your God.**
>
> **—Numbers 10**

The Lord remembers us when we praise Him and pray to Him. It is possible to go through all of the activities of the churches, and then forget to worship the Lord and beseech His help. Prayer comes even before the ministry of the Word! (Acts 6:4).

The Glory of God will be present among us when we pray.

> **13 It came to pass, as the trumpeters and singers *were* as one, to make one sound to be heard in praising and thanking the LORD; and when they lifted up their voice with the trumpets and cymbals and instruments of music, and praised the LORD, *saying,* For *he is* good; for his mercy *endureth* for ever: that *then* the house was filled with a cloud, *even* the house of the LORD;**
>
> **14 So that the priests could not stand to minister by reason of the cloud: for the glory of the LORD had filled the house of God.**
>
> **—II Chronicles 5**

If such worship and praise went up to God under the old covenant, what should worship and praise be like under the new covenant!

The voice of the prophet was employed as the trumpet of God to show the Israelites their sins, and to warn them of the consequences of sin against the Lord their God.

> **1 CRY aloud, spare not, lift up thy voice like a trumpet, and shew my people their transgression, and the house of Jacob their sins.**
>
> **—Isaiah 58**

The close relationship between the convocation of Trumpets, the Day of Atonement, and the coming judgment and deliverance (redemption) of the earth and its peoples, can be seen in the trumpet of the Jubilee.

> **9 Then shalt thou cause the trumpet of the jubile to sound on the tenth *day* of the seventh month, in the day of atonement shall ye make the trumpet sound throughout all your land.**
>
> **10 And ye shall hallow the fiftieth year, and proclaim liberty throughout *all* the land unto all the inhabitants thereof: it shall be a jubile unto you; and ye shall return every man unto his possession, and ye shall return every man unto his family.**
>
> **—Leviticus 25**

We are being raised up into the fullness of God's purposes in Christ Jesus, particularly those purposes which have to do with the total destruction of Christ's enemies and the judgment and deliverance of the nations of the earth.

The concepts associated with the blowing of the trumpet have direct bearing upon the Kingdom purposes of the Lord God. The convocation of Trumpets is the New Year's Day of doing business in the Kingdom of God. We are emerging from the ecclesiastical forms of religion and are coming into the union of the spiritual and the material in such a way that the material realm is being brought under subjection to the Lord Jesus Christ.

The Kingdom of God shall have been established when God's will is being done in the earth (the material realm) as it is in heaven (the spiritual realm).

The earth is always governed by spiritual forces. The purpose of the redemption in Christ Jesus is to change the governing spiritual forces from those of wickedness to those of righteousness.

The trumpet, as mentioned in the Scriptures, is related to spiritual warfare. The next convocation after Pentecost is Trumpets. After we have received the baptism of the Holy Spirit we are to enter into battle against the Lord's enemies. The greatest battle, Armageddon, is yet ahead, and is associated with the return of the Lord Jesus from Heaven. That battle will result in the destruction of the armies of wickedness and in the establishment of the Kingdom of God upon the earth.

Every Christian has Christ in his heart. Each time we are willing to go through the death that the Lord requires, and the accompanying resurrection, Christ is strengthened in the inner man. If we cooperate with the Holy Spirit, this process of death, resurrection, and strengthening of our inner spiritual nature will continue until Christ is reigning within us in complete power and glory.

We consent voluntarily to Christ's Lordship. It is not that we lose our own will. Rather, it is that His will and our will are ground together in the mill of tribulations until the two wills become one.

In this sense, the Day of the Lord and the consequent Millennium have their beginning in the heart of each saint. There is coming a Kingdom-wide Day of the Lord and a Kingdom-wide Millennial Jubilee. But the true essence and quality are obtainable now to "whosoever will." The personal fulfillment in our life of the convocation of Trumpets brings us into our personal day of the Lord, our personal rule of Christ.

Holy Spirit-empowered prayer and praise play a large role in our experience of the spiritual fulfillment of the Feast of Tabernacles, which is the third death and resurrection that we encounter in the program of redemption. We cannot stand up under the pressures which are brought to bear upon us as we are being pruned back, and still further back, unless we are willing to keep on praising the Lord, and praying instead of fainting. "Men ought always to pray rather than faint"!

We are tempted to blame other people, and to grumble and complain, as the Lord brings us through the fires of judgment. We have to keep on seeking His face in prayer and keep praising God for His faithfulness, even when we cannot see the end of the tunnel. Otherwise, we are going to be defeated just before the fullness comes.

There is no way to enter the land of promise, the fullness of Christ, other than through spiritual warfare. God does the fighting when we come out of Egypt, but we do the fighting in order to enter into Canaan.

These climactic spiritual battles cannot be fought by people who are alive in their own wills, their own ambitions, their own preeminence, their own plans and ways. The battles of God can be fought only by those who have been through death and resurrection in the Lord God. Jordan represents the third death of redemption, and the land of promise is the third resurrection.

We have come to the end of all that we are attempting to be, and now are ready to accept the sufferings of Christ. The Lord's army is comprised of warriors who have died and been raised in God.

Because they have been resurrected, in this spiritual sense, they are invincible. The second death has no authority over them. They fall on the sword, the Word of God, and cannot be wounded. The sword already has performed its final work in them. They can be hurt no longer. They are free in the Son and alive eternally.

> **14 These shall make war with the Lamb, and the Lamb shall overcome them: for he is Lord of lords, and King of kings: and they that are with him *are* called, and chosen, and faithful.**
>
> **—Revelation 17**

We are "called" in the first death and resurrection. We are "chosen" in the second death and resurrection. We are proven "faithful" in the third death and resurrection.

The army of Christ is going to descend with Him against the wicked forces of the earth, judging them and destroying them, and delivering the peoples of the earth from the oppression of the wicked spirits who currently are occupying their vantage points in the heavenlies.

> **1 BLOW ye the trumpet in Zion, and sound an alarm in my holy mountain: let all the inhabitants of the land tremble: for the day of the LORD cometh, for *it is* nigh at hand;**
>
> **—Joel 2**

The trumpet of the Spirit of God is blowing in the churches today. An alarm is sounding throughout Zion, the Body of Christ. The Spirit is not saying to us, Sleep on! Everything is fine! Do not bother to seek the Lord because no matter what happens upon the earth you will not be disturbed during your pursuit of material rewards and advantages.

Rather, the Spirit of God is speaking to us to seek Christ with all our heart, soul, mind, and strength; to stir up our gifts; to pray; to praise; to arm ourselves to suffer in the flesh and to endure hardship as a good soldier of Jesus Christ.

Now is the time for us to allow the Holy Spirit to make us wise and tough spiritually because the Lord Jesus is getting ready to tear down the forces of wickedness in the heavenlies. These forces are not going to be pleased with the removal of their ancient privilege of ruling the earth. We need to stay very close to the Lord Jesus so that we will not lose sight of the Lord during the heat of the conflict.

The Day of Christ is not going to be a dainty era during which we sit on fleecy clouds playing golden harps!

The Day of the Lord, the period when God judges the earth through Christ, Head and Body, is going to be the most terrible intervention of Divine wrath and judgment yet known upon planet Earth—far, far more penetrating and terrifying than the flood of Noah.

The people of Noah's day did not have to bear the sight of the Son of God in the heavens, the innocent Lamb executed without cause, now returning in the fullness of His wrath in order to avenge Himself upon the sinners and the rebellious of the world.

> **2 A day of darkness and of gloominess, a day of clouds, and of thick darkness, as the morning spread upon the mountains: a great people and a strong; there hath not been ever the like, neither shall be any more after it, *even* to the years of many generations.**
>
> **—Joel 2**

Before the Lord Jesus appears, the earth is going to experience a period of apparent security and peace for everyone. There will be one worldwide government, and a Christless religious organization which will work together with the government to keep everyone in control.

Unity and control will be brought about, and war will be absent. The peoples of the earth will be occupied primarily with buying and selling, with marrying and giving in marriage. They will assume that peace and prosperity have come to stay. But it will be a time of peace and prosperity apart from Jesus Christ.

Then, as a thief in the night, the Lord Jesus is going to appear. All who have made a covenant with Him and have accepted Him as their Savior and lawful King are going to be caught up to meet the Lord in the air. This catching up will usher in a frightful period of violence and destruction.

Can you imagine the reaction of the rulers of the earth, and that of the peoples under their administration, when all realize that Jesus Christ actually is the Son of God and the rightful ruler of the earth?

If Christ never did anything other than appear in the clouds and call out His own, the nations of the earth would destroy themselves in their wrath and frustration. However, they are not going to have that opportunity. Judgment is going to be brought upon them through the Lord and His army.

There are several passages of Scripture which emphasize the fact that the Day of Christ is going to be a period of darkness upon the earth. One of the more prominent of these passages is found in Isaiah.

> **2 For, behold, the darkness shall cover the earth, and gross darkness the people: but the LORD shall arise upon thee, and his glory shall be seen upon thee.**
>
> **—Isaiah 60**

The darkness of the Day of Christ is as the morning dawn spread upon the mountains, a time of thick mists. So it is that the coming of Christ will be as the morning sun arising to burn away the mists and bring the light of the Day of God.

We notice the same description in Zephaniah:

> **15 That day *is* a day of wrath, a day of trouble and distress, a day of wasteness and desolation, a day of darkness and gloominess, a day of clouds and thick darkness,**
>
> **—Zephaniah 1**

Again, we find in the Book of Revelation that this darkness is the judgment of God upon the forces of evil in the earth.

10 And the fifth angel poured out his vial upon the seat of the beast; and his kingdom was full of darkness; and they gnawed their tongues for pain,

—Revelation 16

The concept here is that God is going to pour out His wrath directly upon the "peace and safety" which have been created in the earth apart from the Lordship of His Son. At the climax of this wrath, the Son Himself shall appear with His army of faithful saints. Then will be brought to pass the onslaught described in Joel 2:1–11.

Those who ride with Christ in that Day are "a great people and strong." The world never before has witnessed an army like this. These are the mighty men of the Lord Jesus Christ. They are "called, chosen, and faithful." God has proved them by trial in every manner conceivable.

The training has not been an easy one. Like Joseph of old, they are shut up in prison for a long period of time while they are being tested by the Word of the Lord.

David's mighty men were formed and bound to him in the wilderness before Saul died in battle. The mighty men of the Lord Jesus are being formed and bound to Him right now, in this time, so that they may be prepared to ride with Him at His appearing.

The Lord Jesus and His army will descend from Heaven upon an earth which has achieved peace and prosperity under the ungodly rule of a government which has rejected the Lord Jesus Christ.

The land is as the garden of Eden before them, meaning that all the fair works of the flesh are in their path. They could inherit these if they wished! But the sons of God will accept none of these works because the stench of sin and the flesh is upon them.

The flaming judgment of God proceeds out from the members of the Body of Christ. They leave behind them a burning desolation. Before the members of the Body of Christ can rebuild the earth, the works of the flesh must be ploughed under.

Nothing shall escape the army of Christ. When Israel invaded Canaan they won some excellent initial victories. But soon their will to conquer began to weaken as they met determined resistance from the Philistines.

This will not be the case with Christ's soldiers. They have been trained, trained, trained, by the Holy Spirit. They are tough, well-disciplined, organized in the Spirit to perfection. They will follow Christ and none other.

Christ's soldiers possess His love of righteousness and hatred of iniquity. They are invincible, and they have an unconquerable desire to please Christ. They never will show mercy to the enemies of God. They cannot be stopped or appeased. On and on they march until every enemy of Christ has been judged and destroyed.

> **4 The appearance of them *is* as the appearance of horses; and as horsemen, so shall they run.**
>
> **—Joel 2**

The army of the Lord is a mobile striking force. Their charge is that of a cavalry. The horses are spiritual creatures and transport their riders with speed and strength unparalleled in the material realm.

There are other passages where the same vision is described:

> **15 Thou didst walk through the sea with thine horses, *through* the heap of great waters.**
>
> **—Habakkuk 3**

> **14 And the armies *which were* in heaven followed him upon white horses, clothed in fine linen, white and clean.**
>
> **—Revelation 19**

God's horses of war are as fierce as their riders!

> **24 He swalloweth the ground with fierceness and rage: neither believeth he that *it is* the sound of the trumpet.**
>
> **—Job 39**

The appearing of Christ with His mighty men shall occur with the sound of a furious onslaught.

> **5 Like the noise of chariots on the tops of mountains shall they leap, like the noise of a flame of fire that devoureth the stubble, as a strong people set in battle array.**
>
> **—Joel 2**

Christ shall descend from heaven as the advance of a roaring fire that consumes everything and everyone in its path.

> **8 In flaming fire taking vengeance on them that know not God, and that obey not the gospel of our Lord Jesus Christ:**
>
> **—II Thessalonians 1**

The world will have established a well-developed culture and imposing institutions under the auspices of the lords of darkness. But the culture and institutions will possess none of the saving Presence of Christ in them. Therefore, they all shall be destroyed at the appearing of the Lord and His saints.

Israel was organized into an army in preparation for its invasion of Canaan. The members of the Body of Christ are being organized today by the Holy Spirit in preparation for the invasion of the earth. The Body of Christ will become a "strong people set in battle array."

Anyone who is under the impression that the members of Christ's army are weak, silly do-gooders has no concept of the Divine strength and fury which is being created in the innermost being of God's saints in this very hour.

David had many extraordinary mighty men in his army. Notable among them were the Gadites.

> **8 And of the Gadites there separated themselves unto David into the hold to the wilderness men of might, *and* men of war *fit* for the battle, that could handle shield and buckler, whose faces *were like* the faces of lions, and *were* as swift as the roes upon the mountains;**
>
> **—I Chronicles 12**

The Gadites exemplify several characteristics which are being created in the saints in this present hour. First of all, they were separated unto David, that is, they gave themselves wholly unto their Lord.

The Gadites did not attempt to satisfy both Saul and David so that they would be accepted by whichever side prospered. They declared themselves. They went out into the wilderness with David.

The true saints of God always have to go outside the camp with Christ, bearing His reproach. In one way or another, this will happen to each one of us.

Christ is "in the wilderness" today, and King Saul (the flesh) is on the throne. Saul put up with the growing popularity of David as long as Saul profited and was not injured in any way. But soon his true murderous instincts for preeminence revealed themselves.

So it is today that organized Christianity may accept the gifts of the Holy Spirit. But in the days to come, as the Body of Christ begins to emerge from the Saulish sectarian structures, the true nature of all sectarianism will come out of hiding and show itself to be the murderer of Jesus Christ.

How many religious organizations possess the pure desire to allow the Holy Spirit to exalt Christ to preeminence in the Body of Christ?

The Gadites were men of might. The saints of today are being made strong in the Lord and in the power of His might. The strength of the saints is the strength of faith and holiness. By many methods of His own selecting, the Holy Spirit is guiding us into ever-increasing faith and strength in Christ. Little by little we are maturing in the ability to resist the flesh, the world, and the adversary.

We are gaining skill in using the shield of faith to quench the fiery darts of the wicked one. We are learning to pray, to praise, to meditate in the Word, to look to Jesus for solutions instead of to other people. We are not as easy to put down or to deceive as when we were first saved. We are learning to lean upon the wisdom and strength of the Lord Jesus.

The Gadites were men of war, fit for the battle. They always were prepared for war. They were skillful in warfare.

We Christians are being alerted by the trumpet of the Lord. We understand that we are being prepared for the conflict of the ages. To this end we are learning to endure hardship as good soldiers of Jesus Christ. We are refusing to entangle ourselves with the affairs of this life.

The Gadites could handle shield and buckler. They were excellent in defending themselves against thrusts of the sword.

Many times each day there are thrusts of the enemy aimed at us. As the Lord teaches us, we learn how to parry each thrust.

Hard words from the world, harsh treatment from Christian people, we learn to turn all this aside in the Lord.

Christ sets a table before us in the presence of our enemies, and we are enabled to look only to Jesus and to forget those who would do us harm. We may live in an ocean of envy, but we ignore it and press forward with our eyes fixed upon Christ Jesus.

The faces of the Gadites were like the faces of lions. The saints who ride behind Jesus will have that same kingly, unconquerable bearing; that same ferocity of countenance which will characterize His appearance.

This is not a consortium of kindly philosophers. These are the Lord and His mighty men, and they are intent upon the establishing of the Kingdom of God upon the earth. The soldiers of Christ have endured very rugged training under the watchful eye of the Lord God. Now their hour has come!

The conquering saints have one objective, and that is to please Jesus Christ and to bring all power into subjection to Him. They will show no mercy upon the rebellious and sinful. All whom they confront will either receive the rule of Christ or will be destroyed. There will be no softness nor wavering in their attack upon sin.

The Gadites were as swift as the roes upon the mountains. Jesus charged some of His listeners with being slow to believe. There is a sluggishness of understanding which characterizes people who nominally are Christians but who are still longing for the things of this world. They are slow to move, slow to believe, slow to receive, slow to learn, when it comes to spiritual warfare.

Such is not the case with Christ's mighty men. They are swift to obey, swift to believe, swift to learn, swift to hear the voice of Christ and to move in savage fury against the enemy.

The army of Christ will move with a speed not attainable in the material world. Their descent from Heaven with Christ will come upon the earth with such speed and force that no power available to the ungodly will have any chance at all of slowing their charge. It is the end of the kingdom of darkness, but deliverance and peace to those of the earth who are willing and obedient.

6 Before their face the people shall be much pained: all faces shall gather blackness.

—Joel 2

When the conviction of the Holy Spirit comes upon people they appear to be in pain. Their faces reveal their inner torment. This very conviction and pain will be multiplied many times during the appearing of Christ.

Like Judas of old, the peoples of the earth will hurl down the gold and silver for which they were willing to trade Christ. But, as in the case of Judas, it will be too late. The doors of mercy will be eternally closed to them. The frightful fate of Judas will be theirs. The rebellious will rage against God in that Day, and the screams of anguish will be a thousand times worse than in the time of Noah. But it will be too late for changes to be made! The year of the Lord's redeemed has arrived!

7 They shall run like mighty men; they shall climb the wall like men of war; and they shall march every one on his ways, and they shall not break their ranks:

—Joel 2

These saints will be they who have allowed God to deal with them until their own strength has been brought down to total weakness. They have been faithful unto the death which God has required and they have denied themselves to this point. Therefore, God has placed within them His eternal strength. They can run and never grow weary of running. They can walk and never become tired. They possess within themselves the inexhaustible, eternal strength of God Almighty.

They have learned how to climb obstacles in the Lord. While people are blaming other people and God for their problems, the members of the Lord's army have been taught to look only to Christ for the solution to each problem, no matter how great or how small that problem may appear to be.

Christ's men waste no time grumbling about their circumstances or blaming others. They bring each matter to the Lord Jesus. Through Him they are given the wisdom and power to surmount each difficulty. They will carry this and all other trainings given to them by the Lord into the Day of battle which is coming.

Each one of Christ's soldiers marches on his way. He has learned the voice of the Spirit and he does not make side excursions into areas which interest him but are of no profit to Christ. He has learned to follow the Spirit each day with utter concentration.

He is not easily led off the track. When he is, the Lord reproves him and leads him back to the way of truth. There is no place among the ranks of Christ's soldiers for people who can be led aside from the mission which is before them. They come straight on and their concentration is terrible to behold.

They do not break ranks. They do not allow the enemy to penetrate their wall at any point as he attempts to get a wedge in and hit some Christians from the side or back. These soldiers have had created in them such a holy wisdom and Divine hatred of sin that evil is destroyed at whatever point it comes against them.

No matter how fierce the defense against them becomes they do not stop. They have learned deep in their spirit that Christ is invincible. They trust Christ with their very life and being, as well as with their eternal salvation in God's Presence. Therefore they cannot be frightened into giving way.

They have come to realize that God will always support the Word of Christ and that there is no other power as great as that of Christ. As a result their ranks never break or weaken. They are an irresistible tide of fury rolling across the earth—a global holocaust. This is Christ and His army!

> **8 Neither shall one thrust another; they shall walk every one in his path: and *when* they fall upon the sword, they shall not be wounded.**
>
> **—Joel 2**

One of the principal devices of the enemy is to tempt Christians to thrust one another. Not only are there a thousand divisions in the Body of Christ, but within each local assembling the envy, jealousy, criticizing, backbiting, goes on continuously.

The Holy Spirit is teaching us today concerning the perfect unity of the Body of Christ. In the first place, He instructs us that all divisions in the Church are of the flesh, no matter how "correct" a sectarian creed may be. In the second place, the Holy Spirit is commanding us to cease from all criticizing of each other. We are not permitted to blame, criticize or otherwise find fault with each other.

Freedom from criticizing other people can be a difficult place in Christ to achieve, but it is absolutely necessary if we expect to ride with Christ in that Day. We simply are not allowed to find fault with our brethren.

Whatever evil is directed toward us by the world or by Christians, we are to take to the Lord. We gain the victory over each problem through Christ's wisdom and strength. Sometimes it becomes necessary for us to speak up and defend ourselves. In such cases the Lord will lift us up out of the realm of criticizing and hatred and will help us to be true Christians. In most instances we are better off asking the Lord to take care of the evil which is attempting to wound our spirit.

The members of the Lord's army do not thrust each other under any provocation. They move as one in Christ, having learned how to look only to Him for the solution to every problem, for the healing of every wound. They do not blame other people.

Each soldier of Christ has learned to walk in his own path. There are many experiences in life which are lawful, as far as a Christian is concerned, but there is only one perfect will of God for the moment. The will of God extends down to the smallest detail of our lives. Either we are in prayer at any given moment and seeking the will of the Spirit, or else we are living carelessly according to our own impulses and notions.

The true son of God walks straight on in the Spirit, praying over each step that he takes, continuing in supplication and thanksgiving. There is a perfect path for each Christian. It is our responsibility to look to the Lord Jesus each moment concerning our being in the center of His will in all matters.

The Word of God, the sword of the Holy Spirit, tries, tries, tries our way, tries our deeds, tries our words, tries our motives, tries our imaginations. The sword of the Word cuts deeply into us, dividing asunder the soul and spirit, the joints and marrow. The thoughts and intents of our heart are revealed. Every part of our being must be tried by the Divine fire so that only the gold of His Substance remains. Then when we ride with the Lord in that Day, the sword of judgment can no longer wound us.

The Day of the Lord is the day of judgment of all spirits and people. The sword of the Spirit will turn this way and that, piercing and slaying all in its path. The army of Christ can fall on the sword and not be wounded. In fact, even the second death, the lake of fire, has no harmful effect upon them. They have been crucified with Christ and it is Christ Who is living in them. Neither sword nor fire can in any manner harm the Lord Jesus Christ!

> **9 They shall run to and fro in the city; they shall run upon the wall, they shall climb up upon the houses; they shall enter in at the windows like a thief.**
>
> **—Joel 2**

The evil forces of the end time will rule from the great cities of the earth, or perhaps all the cities will be combined into one great city. It seems likely that the frightful judgments of the last days will be poured out upon the cities, upon the headquarters of the rule of Antichrist and the apostate church.

The Lord and His army are going to invade these centers of demon rule. They shall tear down every wall, every defense, which men will erect against Christ's appearing. The sons of God will enter into every home, judging the inhabitants concerning their attitude toward the Lord Jesus Christ.

In the horror stories with which we entertained ourselves as children, there are descriptions of monsters coming up to our windows and peering in. We shrieked in horror at the imaginary sight of wierd faces grimacing at us as we huddled in our houses in terror.

The reverse of this will come to pass during the Day of the Lord. The practitioners of every ungodly, filthy, demoniacal wickedness will be cowering in their houses in that Day. Then at the windows of their dwellings will appear what will be to them the most tormenting sight in the universe—the faces of God's saints radiating a pure light as bright as the sun. The Divine brightness will expose every filthy practice, every unclean deed, word and fantasy in which the demon-possessed revel.

The peoples of the earth are already practicing filthy works in their houses which the saints are not allowed even to mention. In that Day this filth will have reached its climax. The Spirit-filled saints of the Lord will break into every dwelling, bringing the Divine light into these private moral cesspools.

The demon-possessed will crouch in their dark corners in terror, just as the demons screamed in fright whenever Jesus of Nazareth came close to them. Their houses may be barricaded in those days, but the righteous will break into the privacy like thieves.

> **10 The earth shall quake before them; the heavens shall tremble: the sun and the moon shall be dark, and the stars shall withdraw their shining:**
>
> **—Joel 2**

So great will be the onslaught of Christ and His army that the earth will shake. The heavens also shall tremble. The army of Christ will affect not only the wickedness in the earth but in the heavens as well. Every person, spirit and thing in the universe, physical and spiritual, will tremble when the army of the Lord begins its march. All acts of men and of angels will be brought into judgment.

Absolutely nothing will be able to stand before the advance of this army. It is the Avenger of all of the sin and rebellion against God which has ever occurred. The army is filled to overflowing with the power and fire of judgment. God has turned over to it the execution of His wrath and the army is instantly obedient to God.

The sun, moon and stars shall cooperate with the saints by ceasing to give their light, just as in the time of Joshua. Darkness will cover the earth, but the light coming from the sons of God will be as many suns. The darkness of the earth will bring into stark contrast the distinction between that which is holy and that which is unholy, that which is clean and that which is unclean. The only light in the world in that Day will be the Divine light of Christ radiating from His invading troops.

> **11 And the LORD shall utter his voice before his army: for his camp *is* very great: for *he is* strong that executeth his word: for the day of the LORD is great and very terrible; and who can abide it?**
>
> **—Joel 2**

Christ is going to shout out from the mouths of His troops, just as a mighty man gives his battle cry. The Lord shall roar out of Zion in anticipation of the battle. They who are riding with Him are called, chosen, and faithful. The "camp" of the Lord is very great. Remember that God promised Abraham that his Seed (Christ) would be in number as the "stars of the heaven." Scientists inform us that the number of stars is very great.

There are many saints in the Lord's army, saints who have been prepared by the Lord from the time of the creation of mankind. Truly it is a great host, some of the soldiers already having had thousands of years of experience in the knowledge of Jesus Christ. Each warrior has been tested in every area and has proven to be faithful.

God the Father has assigned all authority and power in heaven and upon the earth to His beloved Son, the Lord Jesus Christ. This authority and power is resident in the Lord's army. Nothing in heaven or upon the earth will be able in any manner whatever to withstand the march of the army whose Commander-in-chief has the full support of God the Father.

The Day of the Lord indeed will be both "great and very terrible." The only persons who will be able to endure the terror of that Day will be those who have made their covenant with God through the blood of Jesus Christ. Only they who have obeyed God will be able to survive the onslaught of the Lord Jesus and His troops.

The Spirit is testifying that the marching orders are soon to be given to Christ and His army.

5

Preparation for War

We can learn many things about preparing for war from the Book of Joshua.

> **5 And Joshua said unto the people, Sanctify yourselves: for to-morrow the LORD will do wonders among you.**
>
> **—Joshua 3**

The Word and the Spirit are telling us that God is going to do great things. It is an hour of preparation.

Sanctify yourselves! Sanctify yourselves! Sanctify yourselves!

There come times in the history of the Kingdom of God when God is ready for a major step forward. In order to be prepared for God's move we must sanctify ourselves, we must set ourselves apart unto God's Person, purpose, plan, and ways.

We must address ourselves with renewed determination to the serving of the Lord. We must repent, putting out of our lives all that is not holy. Those things which we are doing which are merely good must give place to that which is the best of which we are capable.

Today is one such time. God is ready to perform wonders in the heavens and upon the earth. The Spirit of God is exhorting us and warning us to turn to the Lord with the greatest diligence of which we are capable.

All sin must be put away. We must forsake all competing and distracting interests, ambitions, plans, and desires, take up our cross, and follow the Lord Jesus Christ.

If we thus prepare ourselves we will be ready for the world-wide harvesting of souls which is at hand. But if we do not prepare ourselves we will fall into the snares of the devil, because very great tribulation and temptation are at hand.

We must watch and pray! watch and pray! watch and pray so that we may be able to stand in the Presence of the Son of Man! To be able to stand spiritually throughout the shakings which are coming upon both the spiritual and material realms will require total consecration to Jesus Christ. Jesus will provide us with the wisdom and strength to go from victory to victory throughout earth's darkest hour.

When gross darkness covers the peoples of the earth, then the light of God's Spirit will arise upon the saints.

> **6 And Joshua spake unto the priests, saying, Take up the ark of the covenant, and pass over before the people. And they took up the ark of the covenant, and went before the people.**
>
> **—Joshua 3**

God is speaking to His leaders and teachers today. We are to set an example to the Lord's saints. Whatever we preach we are required to do. We cannot expect the people to quit sinning and to take up their cross until we quit sinning and take up our cross.

It is up to God's preachers to "pass over before the people." There is to be no more money-making, no more seeking our own advantage and gain, from the Gospel of the Kingdom. We are to lay down our own lives so that the resurrection life of Jesus Christ might enter into those who hear us.

The Ark of the Covenant represents the Presence and will of God, the testimony of His holiness and righteousness in Christ.

> **7 And the LORD said unto Joshua, This day will I begin to magnify thee in the sight of all Israel, that they may know that, as I was with Moses, *so* I will be with thee.**
>
> **—Joshua 3**

God has richly anointed and blessed the ministries of the Christian Church as they have labored throughout the centuries. Multitudes of people have made their peace with God through the Lord Jesus Christ. There have been a few individuals, at least, who have pressed on past the rudiments of salvation and have found their joy in living in the Spirit of God.

They have come into a fuller relationship to Jesus Christ than has been true of the majority of believers.

In addition, the Christian Gospel has inspired social reform and works of mercy in many areas of human life, such as the improvement of the educational opportunities of all children, nursing care, abolition of slavery, prison reform, providing for the poor, and so forth. In numerous instances, Christian people can be found at the heart of benevolent, humane enterprises.

God indeed has magnified the spiritual and social works which have labored in the name of the Lord Jesus Christ.

But ours is a new day. The Kingdom of God is at hand. That which was envisioned by the prophets of Israel is soon to come to pass in the earth.

We are witnesses of what happens when mankind trusts in its own education and achievements, apart from the Lord God. Wars, famines, rape, perversion, murder, hatred, and every other abomination fill the earth. The harder man works apart from God to achieve peace and abundance, the more he is denied peace and abundance. In the meanwhile, the humble of the earth who trust in the Lord find peace and the supplying of their needs.

The abomination which produces desolation is here already. Man is making himself god. 666 is the trinity of man—man making himself god.

Whenever man makes himself god, such as in the religion of Humanism, the inevitable result is desolation—spiritual, moral, financial, intellectual and artistic impoverishment.

We of the "civilized" nations are approaching the midnight hour. The wheat and the tares are growing toward maturity. Christ and Antichrist are heading toward the ultimate confrontation.

God has provided a ministry for today which will make the true believers more than conquerors in Jesus' name. The fullness of this slowly-developing ministry is portrayed in symbolic form by the two witnesses of Revelation, Chapter 11.

Christ will roar through His Body in a voice of thunder—a trumpet blast issuing from the saints which will shake the heavens and the earth. The Lord Jesus will warn both His Church and the world of the nearness of His Presence. The Day of Wrath is close at hand. All the world is to repent of wicked practices and believe the Good News that the Kingdom of God is soon coming to the earth.

It is true that the midnight hour is approaching. All of the works of men will be exposed as the pitiful gaspings and gropings which indeed they are.

Then the Lord God of Heaven will display before the amazed vision of the creatures of Heaven and earth the utter folly of existence apart from His glorious Presence and blessing.

Jesus is coming soon! In preparation for His coming, the Lord is issuing to His elect wisdom and power without precedent in the history of mankind. "Greater works than these shall ye do"!

"This day will I begin to magnify thee in the sight of all Israel."

We have witnessed the blessing of God upon the Christian enterprises of the past and present. But now "Moses is dead"! God is "speaking to Joshua." The Lord is enlarging the dimension of militancy, of spiritual warfare, which is part of the Body of Christ, the Wife of the Lamb.

The spiritual control of the world will not be yielded by Satan and his followers without a fierce, vicious struggle. The armies of Hell consider the earth and its peoples to be their own inheritance, not the inheritance of Jesus Christ and His saints.

Therefore, we are now in the Levitical convocation of Trumpets, to speak in terms of a Scriptural type (Leviticus 23:24). It is the time of spiritual warfare. It is the hour of Jubilee, of release from the tyrant who has held the peoples of the earth in spiritual chains and slavery (Leviticus, Chapter 25). Satan and every one of his followers are to be driven out of the earth, out of the peoples of the earth.

> **1 THE earth is the LORD'S, and the fulness thereof; the world, and they that dwell therein.**
>
> **—Psalms 24**

What right do Satan and his angels have to keep on destroying the inhabitants of the earth, to keep on bringing the curse of God upon the inheritance of the Lord Jesus Christ?

We Christians are being trained to fight in the conflict of the ages. We were called by the Lord Jesus, we have been chosen because we responded wholeheartedly to the call, and now we are being proven to be faithful as we serve the Lord in difficult and vexing circumstances which are testing our patience.

The war has commenced already. Are *you* standing against the enemy in your assigned place?

The ultimate confrontation will be the Battle of Armageddon. That is the battle in which Christ attacks Antichrist and destroys him out of the earth.

Today, the Lord Jesus, in anticipation of Armageddon, is beginning to confront His people with the realities of spiritual warfare. Every day we are presented with a new challenge, a new lesson to learn. Is that true in your life? And we *are* learning!

We can see that the God of Heaven is "magnifying" this new dimension of Jesus Christ. Christ is becoming to us the Lord of Armies. We are beginning to perceive the enormous authority and power of the galactic Christ—authority and power which control Heaven, earth, and the spiritual prisons in the interior of the earth, referred to several times in the Scriptures.

We have not passed this way heretofore. *Change* is upon us. The Kingdom of God is at hand. The authority and power to totally crush Satan under our feet was designated as belonging to us by the Lord Jesus. It was gained upon the cross of Calvary; and it will be utterly, totally, absolutely demonstrated throughout the universe as the Kingdom of God is exercised in the victorious saints, in the entire Church, and finally in every creature in the heavens and upon the earth.

The conflict of the ages in all of its fury is upon us. The cross of Jesus Christ is leading on before. The soldiers of the cross are standing up for Jesus.

Will *you* stand in your place "round about the camp"?

6

You Can Be An Overcomer!

We have been pardoned by God the Father when we believe upon Jesus Christ. Now what do we do? Do we wait until we die so that we can escape from the pain of this life and go to live eternally in Heaven? Or do we set out to gain the Kingdom of God, to attain to the resurrection from the dead?

Is our goal to die and go to Heaven? Or is our goal to live in the fullness of the resurrection power of Jesus Christ?

If the rewards described in the second and third chapters of the Book of Revelation actually are the result and fruit of our behavior now, and are not some kind of gifts which will be handed out to all who believe upon Jesus Christ whether or not they learn to live as saints, then it is important that every believer understand clearly what it means to overcome—to conquer according to the meaning of the second and third chapters of the Book of Revelation.

THE OVERCOMERS*

The term *overcome* refers to a struggle. It is a fight between two personalities, two opposing forces. The one which overcomes is the force which manages to impose its will upon its adversary.

Two *wills* are involved—God's will and Satan's will. God's will is being performed in Heaven. To a certain extent, Satan's will is being performed in the earth. The Kingdom of God is

---

*Jim McKeever's new book *You Can Overcome* (Omega Publications, P.O. Box 4130, Medford, OR 95701) is an outstanding, in-depth work on the Overcomers and how *you* can overcome.

the performing of God's will in the earth as it is being performed in Heaven.

A person believes upon Jesus Christ, is baptized in water, and thus becomes a Christian. His sins are pardoned. God hears his prayers. If he should die he will be saved from the claims of Satan and his demons.

Let us assume that he was saved at the age of twenty and lives to be seventy-five years of age. He acts, speaks, and thinks as a Christian upon the earth for fifty-five years.

How important is it that he act, speak, and think in righteousness, holiness, and obedience to God? Is he limited, in the Christian redemption, to being pardoned while the sins of this world compel him against his will to act, speak, and think in unrighteousness, uncleanness, and disobedience to the God of Heaven?

Does the Lord Jesus Christ save us *from* our sins or *in* our sins?

The question is, is it possible through Jesus Christ to overcome the world, or are we doomed to failure? Does the New Testament teach that we can conquer sin and disobedience to God, or does it teach that as long as we are in this world, sin shall have dominion over us?

The New Testament teaches us very clearly that the Christian redemption includes both pardon and the ability to overcome the power of sin. It teaches also that if we do not overcome sin we stand in danger of very serious loss in the Kingdom of God.

> 14 For sin shall not have dominion over you: for ye are not under the law, but under grace.
> 15 What then? shall we sin, because we are not under the law, but under grace? God forbid,
>
> —Romans 6

> 12 Therefore, brethren, we are debtors, not to the flesh, to live after the flesh.
> 13 For if ye live after the flesh, ye shall die: but if ye through the Spirit do mortify the deeds of the body, ye shall live.
>
> —Romans 8

(Notice how verses 12 and 13—preceding—are set in the context of the resurrection from the dead—8:11!)

Two forces are resisting each other in our lives. The Holy Spirit, and Christ Who has been born in us, are striving to perform the will of the Father. Satan, the world, and our flesh are striving to perform the will of Satan. This is true in our actions, our words, and our thoughts.

Which force will win? Which force will overcome, will conquer? Which force will gain control of our behavior and be displayed in the earth? This is the challenge of Christian discipleship.

It is not a question of who possesses the greater power. Jesus Christ possesses infinitely greater power than Satan.

The question has to do with our faith. *Faith* is the victory that overcomes the world.

If we desire to perform God's will while we are upon the earth, and if we believe that Jesus Christ can and will enable us to perform His will, then we gradually will learn how to conquer our lusts and self-will. Little by little we gain the upper hand, we actually *conquer* the sin and death which is in our flesh and in the world.

The sin and pride in our actions is driven out. The sin and pride in our speech is driven out. Finally, the sin and pride in our motives and imaginations is driven out.

We do not conquer sin and self by our striving, although God expects us to use what strength we have in *choosing* to do His will. The true and eternal victory comes as we cooperate with the Holy Spirit in the total destruction of sin and self-seeking out of our personality.

The Lord Jesus through the Spirit of God is leading us to victory upon victory. Lust is fleeing before the army of the Lord. Lying is being destroyed. Gossiping is being stopped. Fornication is being speared through by the Word of God.

Self-seeking is being crucified. Satan's personality and works are being crushed, cut in pieces, speared through, denounced and mutilated in every conceivable manner, as Christ comes to us in the power of the latter rain.

Through Christ's grace we *are* conquering. We have *chosen* to conquer. The written Word states that we *can* conquer. God is giving us the faith to conquer! conquer! conquer! We are not going to cease until *all* sin of action, *all* sin of speech, and *all* sin of thought, is driven out of the earth.

We are looking for and hoping for a new age in which dwells righteousness of conduct. Is that what you desire? Then have faith in God. God has determined to destroy the works of the devil through Jesus Christ, not only in Heaven, but also upon the earth.

Is that what *you* truly desire? Would you care to live in a world in which there is no sin of any kind? Not even one tiny sin? Not even *your* tiny sin and disobedience to the Father?

If an uncompromising "Yes" roars out of the depths of your personality, then join the ranks of God's conquerors. He has placed His Spirit eternally within you. Let your faith be absolutely strong. You are moving toward perfect and complete victory in the Lord Jesus Christ.

If, however, a timid and fearful "Maybe!" proceeds from your heart, then you need to ask God for faith. The timid and fearful cannot possibly enter into the new Jerusalem.

You are the one who will decide. Satan has no power to overcome you if you choose to serve the Lord. In order to conquer a Christian, Satan must lie to him. Satan must successfully deceive him in one way or another.

Satan must enlist the saint's cooperation, either by lust, or pride, or an incorrect understanding of the written Word, or in some other manner which prevents the believer from choosing to conquer in Jesus' name.

People can be healed from sickness in Jesus' name if they will put their trust in Christ and obey Him. People can be healed from sin in Jesus' name if they will put their trust in Christ and obey Him. Both sickness and sin are works of the devil, although sometimes God uses sickness in order to accomplish His purposes in us. It is not a sin to be sick!

We *can* conquer sin if we will follow Jesus Christ! We can be established in righteousness if we will read what God has written to us and mix faith with what we read. We *can* gain the upper hand over the works of the devil. WE CAN CONQUER!

7

The Day of Atonement

We have just described the relationship of the convocation of Trumpets to the coming of our Lord Jesus Christ and to our riding with Him upon the war horses of God. Now we will examine the events associated with the second event in the Feast of the Tabernacles, the Day of Atonement, which is the sixth in the order of the seven Levitical convocations (Leviticus, Chapter 23).

The Day of Atonement is especially rich in symbolism, in terms of our redemption, because it is number *six*. Mankind was created in the image of God upon the sixth day of creation. Thus the Day of Atonement portrays the crowning work of God in redemption. Therefore, it is placed just before the "rest of God." The rest of God is the full possession of our inheritance and our rest from our enemies.

The Day of Atonement *(Yom Kippur)* is celebrated on the tenth day of the seventh month. It was the only day of the year when the high priest of Israel was allowed into the Holy of Holies. The anointed priest went behind the veil and sprinkled blood upon and before the Mercy Seat to make an atonement for his own sins, and then for the sins of the nation of Israel.

The second great act of the observance of *Yom Kippur* was the confessing of the sins of Israel and the laying of them upon the "scapegoat." The scapegoat then was lead away into the wilderness by a man appointed to that task.

The word *atonement* includes the concepts of covering over sin, of appeasing (propitiating) the wrath of God, of forgiveness, of annulment of debt, of remission of sin, of reconciliation and of healing. Every factor that is necessary for the complete reconciliation of a sinful human being to the holy Lord of Israel is contained in the atonement made through the blood of the Lord Jesus Christ.

The Mercy Seat could be more correctly termed the Lid of Reconciliation. The term *mercy* falls short of describing what is contained in the atonement.

We can have mercy upon someone and let them go their way and ignore them. But God's atonement brings us from chaos of body, soul and spirit all the way to conformation to the image of Jesus Christ and to perfect union with Him. Surely this is more than merely the showing of mercy! This is *reconciliation* in the fullest significance and implication of the term.

Thus, the Day of Atonement is the Day of Reconciliation. It is the day when we are brought wholly into the Presence of God and Christ and when judgment and deliverance is extended through the Church to the nations of the earth.

The Day of Atonement is described in the sixteenth chapter of Leviticus.

> **2 And the LORD said unto Moses, Speak unto Aaron thy brother, that he come not at all times into the holy *place* within the veil before the mercy seat, which *is* upon the ark; that he die not: for I will appear in the cloud upon the mercy seat.**
>
> **—Leviticus 16**

Aaron's two sons had just been slain because they had offered incense in an improper manner before the Lord God. God now was impressing upon Aaron that the sanctity of the Holy of Holies was not to be violated and that any person who dared to behave in a presumptuous manner within the Tabernacle would also be slain. God Himself was dwelling between the wings of the covering cherubim of glory!

> **5 And he shall take of the congregation of the children of Israel two kids of the goats for a sin offering, and one ram for a burnt offering.**
>
> **6 And Aaron shall offer his bullock of the sin offering, which is for himself, and make an atonement for himself, and for his house.**
>
> **—Leviticus 16**

Here is one of the major differences between the priesthood of Aaron and his sons, and the priesthood of Christ. Aaron and his sons had to offer bullocks for their own sins. Christ never had to offer any sacrifice for His own sins because He was without sin. His sacrifice was made for us.

> **7 And he shall take the two goats, and present them before the LORD *at* the door of the tabernacle of the congregation.**
>
> **8 And Aaron shall cast lots upon the two goats; one lot for the LORD, and the other lot for the scapegoat.**
>
> **—Leviticus 16**

There is an extremely important concept revealed in the preceding passage. There were two goats, not just one goat. One goat was offered for a sin offering. It was the Lord's goat. The other goat remained alive and was let go into the wilderness. It was the scapegoat.

These two goats portray the two great dimensions of the atonement. The first occurred upon the cross of Calvary, in which the sin offering was made and the guilt of sin was removed. The second will occur at the coming of our Lord Jesus Christ, in which the presence of sin will be removed from the camp just as the scapegoat was removed. "Unto them that look for him shall he appear the second time without sin unto salvation."

Jesus Christ is not satisfied with propitiating the wrath of God and forgiving sin. He is going to proceed to completely demolish the power of sin and remove it from His Body—a process which already has commenced in the Church.

At His glorious appearing Christ is going to complete the removing of all effects of sin from His Church and then is going to remove sin from the entire earth. His name is Jesus, not because He saves His people *in* their sins but because He saves His people *from* their sins!

The Lord is faithful and just, not only to forgive us our sins, but also to cleanse us from all unrighteousness. The atonement made by Christ includes not only forgiveness but also total deliverance. It is a complete and full reconciliation to all that God desires and to all that God Himself Is.

> **9 And Aaron shall bring the goat upon which the LORD'S lot fell, and offer him *for* a sin offering.**

> **10 But the goat on which the lot fell to be the scapegoat, shall be presented alive before the LORD, to make an atonement with him, *and* to let him go for a scapegoat into the wilderness.**
>
> **—Leviticus 16**

One goat was slain and one lived. Christ died but He rose again. We are baptized not only into His death but also into His resurrection.

Because He lives we are going to be saved to the uttermost, meaning that we are going to be reconciled completely to the Father. There is a part of us which must die upon the cross of Christ. But there is a new creation which is alive forevermore.

Redemption includes not only forgiveness, as marvelous as that is, but also a perfect re-creation and absorption into the Divine Nature. Every guilt, tendency and effect of sin is being removed from us through means of the authority and power of the Divine atonement which has been made through Christ Jesus. Will we allow the Holy Spirit to work a perfect work of atonement in us?

The removal of the scapegoat signifies not only the complete reconciliation of the members of the Body of Christ to God but also the total removal of the presence of sin from the earth. One of the principal missions of Christ, Head and Body, will be the judgment and destruction of all sources and forms of sin in the earth. The planet upon which we now are living is going to be purged of all sin.

Think of it! God is not going to destroy the heaven and the earth until He first demonstrates for one thousand years that He is well able to rule in righteousness upon this earth or in any other area that He chooses. God is never defeated!

After the Lord has demonstrated His power, wisdom, righteousness and compassion with utmost clarity, He is going to cast aside in disdain the entire material creation—the heavens and the earth—and create a new heaven and a new earth.

God will make new creatures and He will not want so much as a dim memory remaining of the sorrow and grief which His Son and the saints have had to endure because of the presence of sin in the heaven and the earth.

12 And he shall take a censer full of burning coals of fire from off the altar before the LORD, and his hands full of sweet incense beaten small, and bring *it* within the veil:

13 And he shall put the incense upon the fire before the LORD, that the cloud of the incense may cover the mercy seat that *is* upon the testimony, that he die not:

—Leviticus 16

The cloud of perfume which arose from the pouring of the holy incense upon the hot coals of the censer was an important part of the observance of the Day of Atonement. The fragrance of the perfume was to "cover the mercy seat." This type was fulfilled when the holy prayers and praises of Jesus of Nazareth ascended to the Father, especially during the time of His crucifixion.

The Kingdom-wide fulfillment of the enveloping of the Mercy Seat in the holy perfume is described in Revelation, Chapter 8. The incense, which is the fragrance of Christ Jesus, is mixed with the prayers of the saints. The whole is poured out on the coals of the golden censer. The holy perfume ascends "up before God out of the angel's hand."

Then the trumpets of the Lord prepare to sound. There will be a great increase in the prayer and praise which ascends from the members of the Body of Christ before God will give the signal for the trumpets to sound, announcing the return of the Lord Jesus.

Christ will appear as the complete fulfillment of the Day of Atonement, the Day of Reconciliation. The trumpets will announce the Millennial Jubilee—the time of the restoration of all things to their rightful owners.

Satan has stolen that which belongs to Christ and His saints, but it will all be returned in the Jubilee. Can you believe that the kingdom of darkness is going to be completely spoiled and those who destroy the earth are going to be destroyed? There is nothing that anyone can do to prevent it. The Day of Atonement is on the way, the Day of Reconciliation, the Day of the completion of redemption.

9 Then shalt thou cause the trumpet of the jubile to sound on the tenth *day* of the seventh month, in the day of atonement shall ye make the trumpet sound throughout all your land.

> **10 And ye shall hallow the fiftieth year, and proclaim liberty throughout *all* the land unto all the inhabitants thereof: it shall be a jubile unto you; and ye shall return every man unto his possession, and ye shall return every man unto his family.**
>
> **—Leviticus 25**

The Day of Christ's appearing is the fulfillment of the Day of Atonement—*Yom Kippur* of the Jews. He is going to appear "without sin unto salvation." The fullness of redemption is yet ahead of us, as so many of the New Testament passages indicate. We Christians now possess the Holy Spirit as the pledge of the Day of Redemption which is yet to come.

The Day of Christ will be the day of perfect reconciliation, deriving its authority from the blood of the cross. The Church will be united with Christ as expressed in the words: "The marriage of the Lamb is come, and his wife hath made herself ready."

All sin will be judged and cast out of the earth. The Lamb and His Wife then will shepherd the earth with a rod of iron. There will be a peace imposed by force which will last for one thousand years. This is the manner in which the world is going to be reconciled to God (II Corinthians 5:19).

The third death and resurrection, in which we have to deny ourselves and be raised up by the power of Christ, is necessary if we are to inherit the fullness of fruit and strength which will bless the nations during the thousand-year fulfillment of the Day of Atonement.

Today, God is looking for saints who will be able to rule with Him and experience this unbounded fruitfulness and dominion. In order for Him to assign such fruitfulness and dominion He first must make us barren of the fruit which we brought forth under other levels of His workings with us. In order for Him to assign such strength He first must make us weak, deprived of the strength which we possessed prior to this deeper pruning.

To those whom God has made barren shall be given the most extraordinary fruitfulness (Isaiah 54:1). To those whom God has made weak shall be given the most extraordinary strength (II Corinthians 12:9).

Their new fruitfulness and strength shall result in their being kings and priests of Christ throughout the Millennial Jubilee and then on through eternity during the new heaven and earth reign of Jesus Christ. "Come, and let us return unto the Lord: for he hath torn, and he will heal us; he hath smitten, and he will bind us up (Hosea 6:1).

> **14 And he shall take of the blood of the bullock, and sprinkle *it* with his finger upon the mercy seat eastward; and before the mercy seat shall he sprinkle of the blood with his finger seven times.**
>
> **15 Then shall he kill the goat of the sin offering, that *is* for the people, and bring his blood within the veil, and do with that blood as he did with the blood of the bullock, and sprinkle it upon the mercy seat, and before the mercy seat:**
>
> **—Leviticus 16**

The atoning blood was sprinkled upon the eastern side of the Mercy Seat, the side facing the land of promise. The blood of Christ looks forward to that perfect day when the Church is married to Him in total and complete union, and the earth is free from sin, having been perfectly reconciled to God.

The blood was sprinkled seven times, signifying that the blood is going to work a perfect work of reconciliation within us. As in the case of Naaman the Syrian, when we come up after the seventh "dip" we shall be healed. We shall be as a little child, ready to enter the Kingdom of God (II Kings 5:14).

We are being redeemed "to the uttermost"! (Hebrews 7:25).

The redeeming blood of Christ keeps on working throughout all areas of redemption. Each of the Levitical feasts included the offering of animals. We overcome through the blood of the Lamb. We are reconciled to God through the blood of Christ.

All through the working out of the phases of our redemption the blood keeps on making up the difference between our actual attainment in holiness and righteousness and the standard of righteous and holy conduct required by God.

We noticed previously that the army which is going to invade the earth from heaven will be led by a Commander-in-chief Who is "clothed with a robe dipped in blood." It is the precious blood of Christ which will make possible the perfect union of the Church with Christ and also the cleansing from sin of the nations of the earth.

The blood of young bulls and goats was sprinkled upon the east side of the Mercy Seat and *before* the Mercy Seat, no doubt indicating that some of the blood fell upon the Ark of the Covenant and some upon the ground in front of the Ark. This was the "reconciling" of the "holy place."

In addition, blood was put upon the horns of the Altar of Incense (Exodus 30:10). This was the reconciling of the "tabernacle of the congregation."

Finally, blood was sprinkled seven times upon the "horns of the altar round about" (Leviticus 16:18). This was the reconciling of the Altar of Burnt Offering which stood in the courtyard of the Tabernacle complex.

Scholars are not in agreement as to whether the "altar" of Leviticus 16:18 refers to the Altar of Incense or the Altar of Burnt Offering. We have come to the conclusion that it refers to the Altar of Burnt Offering.

If we are correct, there occurred the reconciling of the three parts of the Tabernacle: (1) the Holy of Holies, with the sprinkling of the blood upon the Mercy Seat and before the Mercy Seat; (2) the Holy Place, with the putting of the blood upon the horns of the Altar of Incense; and (3) the courtyard, with the seven-fold sprinkling of the blood upon the horns of the Altar of Burnt Offering.

The blood placed upon the Mercy Seat and before the Mercy Seat speaks of the work of reconciliation in the holiest of all. The holiest of all is found in heaven before the very throne of the Father, and also in the innermost being of the saint. The blood sprinkled *before* the Mercy Seat reminds us that the *way* to the throne of God has to be sanctified as well as the throne itself.

The blood placed upon the horns of the Altar of Incense portrays the sanctifying of the prayer and praise which ascends to God from the Church.

The most holy Presence of God is found first in the Lord Jesus Christ. The way to reconciliation with God was opened up for all people when Jesus Christ offered His precious blood upon and before the Mercy Seat in heaven.

Next, perfect holiness is being developed in the hearts of the fervent disciples of the Lord Jesus. The work of Christ in the Church will not cease until it is perfect—a complete counterpart of the Lord Jesus Christ in every way. The reconciling of this "holy place" is made possible through the sprinkling of the blood of Jesus. Otherwise, our worship, supplication and service would not be acceptable before the throne of the Almighty in heaven.

Finally, the sprinkling of the blood upon the Altar of Burnt Offering reveals to us that the purpose of God is to fill the entire earth with the worship of Himself.

> **21 But *as* truly *as* I live, all the earth shall be filled with the glory of the LORD,**
>
> **—Numbers 14**

We learn from the above verse that God, bring provoked by the unbelief of Israel in the wilderness, swore by Himself that He would fill the whole earth with His glory. The filling of the earth with the glory and praise of God appears many times throughout the Old Testament as various prophets gave voice to the burden of the Word of the Lord. This is particularly true of the Psalms.

> **8 Let all the earth fear the LORD: let all the inhabitants of the world stand in awe of him.**
>
> **—Psalms 33**

> **10 Be still, and know that I *am* God: I will be exalted among the heathen, I will be exalted in the earth.**
>
> **—Psalms 46**

> **8 God reigneth over the heathen: God sitteth upon the throne of his holiness.**
>
> **—Psalms 47**

> **10 According to thy name, O God, so *is* thy praise unto the ends of the earth: thy right hand is full of righteousness.**
>
> **—Psalms 48**

The entire sixty-seventh Psalm is devoted to the coming rule of God throughout the entire earth. This will be accomplished during the Day of Reconciliation as administered through the Lord Jesus Christ and the Body of Christ.

> **1 GOD be merciful unto us, and bless us; *and* cause his face to shine upon us; Selah.**
>
> **2 That thy way may be known upon earth, thy saving health among all nations.**
>
> **3 Let the people praise thee, O God; let all the people praise thee.**
>
> **4 O let the nations be glad and sing for joy: for thou shalt judge the people righteously, and govern the nations upon earth. Selah.**
>
> **5 Let the people praise thee, O God; let all the people praise thee.**
>
> **6 *Then* shall the earth yield her increase; *and* God, *even* our own God, shall bless us.**
>
> **7 God shall bless us; and all the ends of the earth shall fear him.**
>
> **—Psalms 67**

It is abundantly clear in the Scripture that God is going to bless the earth through Christ—Head and Body. First, the blood of Christ will work redemption in the Church until the Church itself has been reconciled to God.

Then through the Church God is going to reconcile the entire earth unto Himself. This is the Kingdom-wide Day of Atonement. The reconciliation will have been completed in its entirety by the end of the Millennium. Then the final purging will take place.

The fruit of the reconciliation will be carried over into the new heaven and earth reign of Jesus Christ. Jesus Christ then will behold the fruit of the travail of His soul and will be satisfied. The work which has been accomplished will prosper in God's hand forever and ever, world without end.

The enormous fruit and strength gained by the members of the Body of Christ as the result of the efforts of God will depend upon the willingness of each member of the Body to deny himself and die the death which the Holy Spirit directs for him or her as an individual. God will have it no other way. Jesus Christ Himself is our example, emptying Himself and going to the cross. The result is the fruitfulness and the dominion assigned to Christ.

Now it is our turn. Will we believe Christ and be willing to fall into the ground and die? Are we willing to lose our life? Are we willing to love not our own life unto the death?

If we save our life, we will lose it. If we lose our life for Christ's sake and the Gospel's, then the exceeding fruitfulness and strength will be ours.

Who then is willing to consecrate his service this day unto the Lord?

> **20 And when he hath made an end of reconciling the holy *place*, and the tabernacle of the congregation, and the altar, he shall bring the live goat:**
>
> **21 And Aaron shall lay both his hands upon the head of the live goat, and confess over him all the iniquities of the children of Israel, and all their transgressions in all their sins, putting them upon the head of the goat, and shall send *him* away by the hand of a fit man into the wilderness:**
>
> **22 And the goat shall bear upon him all their iniquities unto a land not inhabited: and he shall let go the goat in the wilderness.**
>
> **—Leviticus 16**

The high priest, as we have stated, reconciled the Holy of Holies, the Tabernacle of the Congregation (Tent of Meeting) and the Altar of Burnt Offering. This threefold application reveals to us that the precious blood of the Lamb will purify the entire Kingdom of God, commencing in the Presence of God in heaven and proceeding downward through the hearts of the saints and out through the earth until the entire heavens and earth have been reconciled to the Father.

> **23 *It was* therefore necessary that the patterns of things in the heavens should be purified with these; but the heavenly things themselves with better sacrifices than these.**
>
> **24 For Christ is not entered into the holy places made with hands, *which are* the figures of the true; but into heaven itself, now to appear in the presence of God for us:**
>
> **—Hebrews 9**

All of the iniquities of the children of Israel were put upon the head of the live goat and it was led away into the wilderness.

All of their transgressions were borne away unto "a land not inhabited." Here is one of the clearest pictures in the Bible of the fact that our sins are not only forgiven by Christ but also are *removed* from us.

Christ did not come just to forgive those of earth who would accept His forgiveness. He came to do that but also to remove from the believers all of the tendencies and effects of sin and finally to judge and destroy all sin and sinners out of the earth.

The Book of I John deals with sin in the Christian life.

> **9 If we confess our sins, he is faithful and just to forgive us our sins, and to cleanse us from all unrighteousness.**
>
> **—I John 1**

Here are the two aspects of the atonement—the forgiveness and the cleansing; the dead goat and the live goat.

There are two major historical works indicated here: (1) Calvary, which had to do with the forgiving of the guilt of sin; and (2) the next appearing of the avenging Christ, which will have to do with the cleansing from all unrighteousness.

We have spoken of the deliverance of the Christian from the guilt and power of sin during our discussion of the second death and resurrection. In the third death and resurrection, that of conquest, the Christian is to endure the self-denial necessary to bring the blessings of forgiveness and deliverance to other people. The third area of redemption will not have been completed until the entire world has been reconciled to God.

We are not teaching that all people will be saved, because there will be some who will not receive Christ as Savior and Lord. These will enter into everlasting torment in which there can be no redemption forever.

Redemption is past, present and future. Past redemption has to do with the forgiveness of sins upon the cross of Calvary. Present redemption has to do with our accepting of the atonement and with our washing our robes and making them white in the blood of the Lamb.

Future redemption has to do with our receiving our glorified bodies and with the judgment and removal of sin from the earth. Future redemption will commence with the appearing of the Lord Jesus from heaven. All of these acts of redemption are fulfillments of *Yom Kippur,* the most sacred day of the Jewish year, the Day of Atonement.

The next coming of Christ will bring to those who look for Him a redemption which is free from every trace of the guilt, tendencies and effects of sin.

If we would be prepared for such a glorious, sin-free salvation, then we must be in the process of purifying ourselves right now. Our time of preparation is described in the following verse:

> **3 And every man who has this hope in him purifies himself, even as he is pure.**
>
> **—I John 3**

Another important area of fulfillment of the Day of Atonement is that of the end-time redemption of the Jewish people. We have referred to this area of reconciliation when discussing the events of the last days. The reconciliation of the Jews with their Messiah will take place during the dark days of the rule of Antichrist. The Body of Christ will be the instrument which the Lord utilizes to restore Jesus Christ to His own family—the children of Israel.

Asenath, the Egyptian bride of Joseph, is a type of the Gentile Wife of the Lamb who will be part of Christ when He reveals Himself to His family.

In order for us to understand how salvation can come suddenly to a group of people, such as the Jews, we first must realize that Christ possesses and can exercise the power and authority to forgive, cleanse and deliver any person whom He will. Our salvation is not by our works but by the grace and election of the Lord. We do not choose Him. He chooses us!

Christ reaches down and saves those whom the Father has given to Him. Of course, when He speaks to us we must obey. If we do not obey, then we run the risk of being among those who are rebels against the Lord and who will be consumed by the fire of eternal judgment.

The concept that Christ can reach down and deliver whom

He will is very important to our understanding if we are to grasp the whole plan of God. We witness the sovereignty of Christ exercised in the case of Lot, who was delivered out of Sodom at the last minute. In this instance, as so often is true, another human being (Abraham) was involved in the exercise of God's sovereign delivering actions.

We can observe the ability of Christ to reach down and save out of darkness, in the incident of Saul on the road to Damascus. Saul was forgiven and commissioned to be an apostle before he had had much time to examine the alternatives. We are not saved by works of righteousness which we have done, but according to the purposes and callings of God.

Paul describes how God in the end time, after leaving them in blindness to His salvation for so many hundreds of years, is going to reach down and redeem the people who are Jewish by natural birth. This is a *very* important fulfillment of the Day of Atonement. It is a sovereign act of reconciliation.

> **25 For I would not, brethren, that ye should be ignorant of this mystery, lest ye should be wise in your own conceits; that blindness in part is happened to Israel, until the fulness of the Gentiles be come in.**
>
> **26 And so all Israel shall be saved: as it is written, There shall come out of Sion the Deliverer, and shall turn away ungodliness from Jacob:**
>
> **27 For this *is* my covenant unto them, when I shall take away their sins.**
>
> **—Romans 11**

Do you see the sovereignty of Christ in the preceding passage? The Deliverer *shall* come and He *shall* turn away ungodliness from Jacob. There are no if's involved here. He *shall* take away their sins.

Christ always retains the power to redeem. He saves whom He will, when He will, by the means which He chooses. The faith to believe in Christ is the gift of God to us. Often Christ invites people to share with Him in prayer, and other forms of service, as He goes about saving those whom He has chosen.

In the end time, Christ is going to demolish all the works

of the kingdom of darkness. He is going to crush Satan under the feet of the Church.

The most important thing right now is that the members of the Body of Christ wash their robes and make them white in the blood of the Lamb. We must confess our sins and receive the pardon and the cleansing.

Next, the members of the Body of Christ must submit to the death of self-denial. After we gain some measure of victory over the world through the Word of God, the Holy Spirit, and the fiery trials which we must undergo, a further reconciliation with God is yet needed. We must become perfectly and totally reconciled to the will of God. Our will must become one with His will.

Those who ride with Christ must be clothed in the sparkling white linen of righteous conduct. Also, the army of saints are as living dead men. They have been crucified with Christ and now Christ is living in them.

When Abraham climbed up Mount Moriah with Isaac at his side he was a living dead man. The 100-year-old patriarch walked with firm step, having a steady hand upon his staff. His path headed straight as an arrow toward the stone altar upon which he was to slay his only son, Isaac. Two thousand years later Abraham's Redeemer, the Lord Jesus, headed straight as an arrow toward Gethsemane and the cross of Calvary, Himself a living dead man.

Abraham's heart was an iron weight within his breast. He was dead while he walked. Life, hope, joy, purpose, reason for living was gone. But the Word of God moved the faithful Abraham toward the mount.

So it will be with those who are to ride with Christ. Each one will have had his personal Mount Moriah and each one will be able to keep on moving under no other power and direction than that of the Word of God. Christ and His army cannot be slain because they have died already. Now they are moved by the Word of God, and the Word of God is indestructible, the mightiest power in the universe.

The redemption of mankind requires two principal actions. First, there must be a full payment of the debt associated with the bondage. The full payment of the debt was made when the blood of Christ was shed upon the cross.

Second, there must be an exercise of force sufficient to destroy the enemy who, being a thief and a robber, will not recognize the payment of the debt but will insist upon keeping his victims in slavery to himself.

The payment of the debt took place two thousand years ago. The exercise of the power of the Holy Spirit in the deliverance from slavery is going on now in those who "through the Spirit do mortify the deeds of the body." Deliverance requires the exercise of superior force. There is relentless warfare going on in the spiritual realm at this present time!

Christ's blood is sufficient not only for the reconciliation of the Church but also for the entire world, if people will receive His mercy and grace.

> **2 And he is the propitiation for our sins: and not for our's only, but also for *the sins of* the whole world.**
>
> **—I John 2**

The sins of the Body of Christ are being removed now as we work with the Holy Spirit in confession, repentance and resistance. At the coming of Christ, the removal of sin will extend to the nations of the earth. The nations will be subjected to the righteous discipline of the rule of the rod of iron. Whoever attempts to rebel against Christ will be judged immediately. The law of the Kingdom of God will be obeyed throughout the earth.

God will not be mocked! The whole earth will be filled with His glory, according to His Word.

How wonderful it would be if Christ would appear and establish His rule today! But first the fullness of Divine life must be developed in the saints. Also, sin must come to full expression (Genesis 15:16). Then Jesus will come and the fulfillment of the Day of Atonement will take place.

Christ is the great High Priest of God. Only He is allowed beyond the veil in heaven. When the time comes to reconcile the whole earth to God, Christ, the Servant of the Lord, will appear as the long-awaited Messiah—the Anointed Deliverer.

The "mystery" of the Gospel is that Messiah is *in* the Church. The Church is the Body of Messiah. When the Head appears, then the Body of Messiah will be joined to the Head. The Head and the Body is the "Servant of the Lord," revealed by Isaiah. The Servant of the Lord is God's instrument of reconciliation.

When Christ appears *in* the Body, and the nation of Israel is reconciled to its rightful King, the Lord Jesus, then the glory of the living God will come upon all Israel.

> **5 Then thou shalt see, and flow together, and thine heart shall fear, and be enlarged; because the abundance of the sea shall be converted unto thee, the forces of the Gentiles shall come unto thee.**
>
> **—Isaiah 60**

All the ends of the earth shall turn unto God Who will be dwelling in Zion (Christ—Head and Body), and Whose glory shall be seen upon Israel, the chosen nation.

The fullness of reconciling glory is portrayed in Ezekiel.

> **9 And it shall come to pass, *that* every thing that liveth, which moveth, whithersoever the rivers shall come, shall live: and there shall be a very great multitude of fish, because these waters shall come thither: for they shall be healed; and every thing shall live whither the river cometh.**
>
> **—Ezekiel 47**

The "waters" are the "living water" which flows from the hearts of the saints. When the saints have been made one in Christ, then the individual streams of living water shall flow together to make the great river of life seen by Ezekiel. The river of life shall flow out to the ends of the earth as the saints go everywhere, bringing to the peoples of the earth the Presence and the ways of the God of heaven.

"Thou hast kept the good wine until now." The coming to the earth of the fullness of God's Spirit is yet ahead, and it will occur at the appearing of our Lord Jesus Christ with His saints. This revival of the Spirit will result in deliverance for all who will receive the rule of the Lord Jesus, but in destruction upon every person who defies Christ.

The era of worldwide deliverance is the fulfillment of the Year of Jubilee (Leviticus, Chapter 25). It is the Millennial Jubilee.

The Day of Atonement occurred on the tenth day of the seventh month. The Feast of Tabernacles took place on the fifteenth through the twenty-second day of the same month (seven days of Tabernacles, and then the designated eighth day). The work of reconciliation associated with the Day of Atonement is the necessary preparation for the eternal indwelling of Christ and the Father associated with the Feast of Tabernacles.

The Millennial Jubilee, the Kingdom-wide fulfillment of the Day of Atonement, is the necessary forerunner of the new heaven and earth reign of Jesus Christ, which is the Kingdom-wide fulfillment of the Feast of Tabernacles.

Tabernacles typifies the rest of God, as God dwells in and with His people. Such rest and abiding is impossible until there has been perfect reconciliation. This is why there must be a Day of Atonement before there is a Feast of Tabernacles, whether we are speaking of one individual, all Israel, or the whole world.

The Day of Atonement is the act of the uniting of the Bridegroom and the Bride. The Feast of Tabernacles is the eternal expression of that perfect union.

8

The Original Feast of Tabernacles

The celebration of Tabernacles was the most joyous occasion of the year. For seven days the Israelites were to sleep out under the stars in booths made of branches. Tabernacles marked the end of the harvest and processing of all the grains, fruits, vegetables and nuts farmed by the Jews. The Law was read. Water from the Pool of Siloam was poured out upon the Altar of Burnt Offering. It was a time of the most extreme hilarity and rejoicing.

One can imagine an Israelite coming out of his house each year and living for a week in a booth made from the branches of trees. Perhaps this was the Lord's way of repeatedly bringing to the attention of the Jews that their most important contribution among the nations of the earth is not to be in the area of government, or economics, or in the arts and sciences, as significant as their contributions in these realms may be.

The most important gift that Israel brings to the family of mankind is the Presence and the Law of the living God.

Also, living in the booths pointed to the day when God dwells in Israel and Israel dwells in God; God rests in Israel and Israel rests in God. The prophets testified of that Day to come, and Jesus and the apostles taught us how God is bringing His plan to pass in human beings. God's plan is Christ *in* us, the hope of glory.

> **34 Speak unto the children of Israel, saying, The fifteenth day of this seventh month *shall be* the feast of tabernacles *for* seven days unto the LORD.**
>
> **35 On the first day *shall be* an holy convocation: ye shall do no servile work *therein*.**
>
> **36 Seven days ye shall offer an offering made by fire unto the LORD: on the eighth day shall be an holy convocation unto you;**

> **and ye shall offer an offering made by fire unto the LORD: it *is* a solemn assembly; *and* ye shall do no servile work *therein*.**
>
> **—Leviticus 23**

The convocation of Trumpets was observed on the first day of the seventh month, *Tishri*. The Day of Atonement took place on the tenth day of *Tishri*. The Feast of Tabernacles lasted seven days, from the fifteenth through the twenty-first of *Tishri*.

Notice the expression, "the eighth day (twenty-second of *Tishri)* shall be a holy convocation unto you" (Leviticus 23:36). The eighth day was a very high Sabbath, celebrated with extraordinary rejoicing. The eighth day of the observance of Tabernacles typifies the first day of the new week of eternity—the week which has no end. The eighth day will find its most complete fulfillment during the new heaven and earth reign of Jesus Christ (Revelation 21:3).

The Feast of the Tabernacles typifies the establishing of the Kingdom of God upon the earth.

Continuing our reading in the twenty-third chapter of Leviticus:

> **39 Also in the fifteenth day of the seventh month, when ye have gathered in the fruit of the land, ye shall keep a feast unto the LORD seven days: on the first day *shall be* a sabbath, and on the eighth day *shall be* a sabbath.**
>
> **—Leviticus 23**

As we mentioned before, the observances of the seven convocations were taught to the Israelites and strictly enjoined upon them while they were wandering in the wilderness between Egypt and Canaan. But the Jews could not celebrate Firstfruits, or Pentecost, or Tabernacles while they were in the wilderness because these convocations have to do with the harvesting of crops. They could not gather in "the fruit of the land" until they were in Canaan. The convocations were given to them in preparation for the time when they were in possession of the land of promise.

This kind of teaching in advance takes place also with us Christians. God is teaching us many, many lessons in the present hour. We are to learn our lessons carefully now for they will be useful to us in the ages to come. Much of what God enjoins upon us at this time will have increasing significance throughout our lifetime upon the earth and even more in the future beyond that.

Each day, as the Holy Spirit directs us, we must apply the lessons which we are learning now. Yet our instruction and preparation is primarily for the Kingdom age and the new heaven and earth reign of Jesus Christ. We will bear much responsibility throughout eternity as God's kings and priests. Is it any surprise, therefore, that we have to be trained so very, very carefully in this present life of our wilderness sojourn?

The celebration of Tabernacles signified the end of the agricultural year and the beginning of the new. All that had been sown in the land had by this time been reaped and processed. The "fruit of the land" included wheat, barley, lentils, peas, beans, onions, millet, grapes, cucumbers, melons, citrus fruits and nuts.

> **40 And ye shall take you on the first day the boughs of goodly trees, branches of palm trees, and the boughs of thick trees, and willows of the brook; and ye shall rejoice before the LORD your God seven days.**
>
> **41 And ye shall keep it a feast unto the LORD seven days in the year. *It shall be* a statute for ever in your generations: ye shall celebrate it in the seventh month.**
>
> **42 Ye shall dwell in booths seven days; all that are Israelites born shall dwell in booths:**
>
> **43 That your generations may know that I made the children of Israel to dwell in booths, when I brought them out of the land of Egypt: I *am* the LORD your God.**
>
> **44 And Moses declared unto the children of Israel the feasts of the LORD.**
>
> **—Leviticus 23**

It was the Lord's intention that the Feast of Tabernacles be a season of great rejoicing over the goodness of the Lord.

> **13 Thou shalt observe the feast of tabernacles seven days, after that thou hast gathered in thy corn and thy wine:**
>
> **14 And thou shalt rejoice in thy feast, thou, and thy son, and thy daughter, and thy manservant, and thy maidservant, and the Levite,**

the stranger, and the fatherless, and the widow, that *are* within thy gates.

15 Seven days shalt thou keep a solemn feast unto the LORD thy God in the place which the LORD shall choose: because the LORD thy God shall bless thee in all thine increase, and in all the works of thine hands, therefore thou shalt surely rejoice.

—Deuteronomy 16

The Feast of Tabernacles was associated with the reading of the law of Moses to the congregation of Israel in solemn assembly.

10 And Moses commanded them, saying, At the end of *every* seven years, in the solemnity of the year of release, in the feast of tabernacles,

11 When all Israel is come to appear before the LORD thy God in the place which he shall choose, thou shalt read this law before all Israel in their hearing.

12 Gather the people together, men, and women, and children, and thy stranger that *is* within thy gates, that they may hear, and that they may learn, and fear the LORD your God, and observe to do all the words of this law:

—Deuteronomy 31

The Feast of Tabernacles was associated also with water. By the latter part of our month of September, the time of the Feast of Tabernacles, the dry season (May through August) is about ended. The early (former) rains are soon to fall. The rivers will begin to flow.

The hard clods of earth, baked by the summer sun, will be moistened so that they can be ploughed in preparation for the sowing of seed of the upcoming farming year. So during the celebration of Tabernacles the Jews were rejoicing not only because of the abundance of the preceding year but also in expectation of the coming of refreshing rains and the hope of the satisfying blessings which the new year might bring to them.

Tabernacles was celebrated for seven days, and then came the eighth day, a high Sabbath, the "great day of the feast." It was the practice, at the time Jesus was on earth, for water to be brought in golden vessels from the Pool of Siloam. Then the high priest poured the water into a basin on the Altar of Burnt Offering.

On the eighth day trumpets were blown and Isaiah 12:3 was sung: "With joy shall ye draw water out of the wells of salvation." It was on this occasion of fervent thanksgiving and jubilation that Jesus stood in the midst and cried, "If any man thirst, let him come unto me, and drink. He that believeth on me, as the scripture hath said, out of his belly shall flow rivers of living water" (John 7:37, 38).

When we read the twelfth chapter of Isaiah, remembering that this passage was closely connected with the celebration of Tabernacles, we realize that the Holy Spirit is teaching us that the Feast of Tabernacles has to do with the abiding of God in Christ in us; and that out from the throne of God in us is going to flow rivers of living water, and that these are waters of eternal life which will one day flow out from the members of the Body of Christ to the farthest reaches of the earth.

> **2 Behold, God *is* my salvation; I will trust, and not be afraid: for the LORD JEHOVAH *is* my strength and *my* song; he also is become my salvation.**
>
> **3 Therefore with joy shall ye draw water out of the wells of salvation.**
>
> **—Isaiah 12**

The fact that God required His people to live in booths for one week out of the year had to do with the special history and mission of the nation of Israel. The Jews were not like the Egyptians, the Babylonians or the Philistines. They were a special called-out nation, a kingdom of priests, the elect of the Lord God Almighty, the recipients of the Divine Testimony—the Ten Commandments.

If an Egyptian, or an Amorite, or a Hittite went out to live in a booth for a week, there was little of national history and significance which he could contemplate other than the accomplishments of the wisdom and energy of his race.

But the Jew could meditate upon the dealings of God with Abraham, Isaac and Jacob; upon the provision which God had made for the perpetuation of their family through the events in the life of Joseph; upon the calling of Moses and the judgments of the Lord upon the gods of Egypt; and then upon the unparalleled miracles which brought them safely out of Egypt and through the wilderness region.

Why would God lay His hand upon one nation of all the nations of the earth and deal with that nation in this remarkable manner? It was something to think about at night, under the stars, as one lay in his little booth of palm and willow branches.

Again, we see the injunction of God upon Israel—in the Sabbath day and in the other holy days—that the people cease for a time their grubbing in the earth and look up in adoration, worship and thanksgiving to the great God Who is interested in and provides for His people.

One of the most important celebrations of the Feast of Tabernacles recorded in Scripture can be found in the eighth chapter of Nehemiah.

It is significant that the occasion is the rebuilding of the Temple in Jerusalem. It is our understanding that the greatest fulfillment of the Feast of Tabernacles will occur at the descending of the holy city, the Wife of the Lamb, upon the great, high mountain of the new earth. At that time there will be the fullest expression of the law of God (the beauty of holiness), eternal water in abundance (the River of Life), and the fullness of light (the glory of God shining forth from the throne of God and of the Lamb).

This will be the coming of the tabernacle of God among men so that He may dwell among them and wipe away all tears.

Reading in Nehemiah, Chapter 8:

> **1 AND all the people gathered themselves together as one man into the street that *was* before the water gate; and they spake unto Ezra the scribe to bring the book of the law of Moses, which the LORD had commanded to Israel.**

All of the gates of the wall of Jerusalem which were rebuilt under Nehemiah are prophetic symbols of the Day of the Lord. In the above verse we see the "water gate," a symbol of the Holy Spirit Who will be outpoured upon the earth during the spiritual fulfillment of the Feast of Tabernacles. That fulfillment is going to come on a grand scale!

Also, it is true in us as individual believers that as Christ is formed and dwells in us the glory of God flows out to other people.

> **2 And Ezra the priest brought the law before the congregation both of men and women, and all that could hear with understanding, upon the first day of the seventh month.**
>
> **—Nehemiah 8**

The reader may recall that the first day of the seventh month was the convocation of Trumpets. Again, we have the prophetic symbolism of the Day of the Lord. The trumpet of God will sound; the glory of God will flow forth; and the laws of the Kingdom of God will be renewed in God's people.

Then through the saints those laws will be carried to the ends of the earth until the Kingdom of Heaven rules the peoples of the earth.

> **7 . . . and the Levites, caused the people to understand the law: and the people *stood* in their place.**
>
> **8 So they read in the book in the law of God distinctly, and gave the sense, and caused them to understand the reading.**
>
> **—Nehemiah 8**

As the Feast of Tabernacles begins to be fulfilled in us, that is, as Christ is formed and dwells in us, we gain increased ability to walk in the ways of the Holy Spirit of God. Our conduct becomes more and more holy.

The next passage presents a concept which is important to us if we are endeavoring to live a victorious life in Christ. The concept is this: if we are to pursue holiness of conduct, under the guidance and enabling power of the Holy Spirit, we are to do so not in grief and gloom but in great joy.

We confess our sins before the Lord and embrace His righteous ways with joy and gladness of heart. With this attitude of joy we become strong in the Lord and thus are enabled to go from step to step in the ascent toward holiness of deed, word, motive and imagination.

> **9 And Nehemiah, which *is* the Tirshatha, and Ezra the priest the scribe, and the Levites that taught the people, said unto all the people, This day *is* holy unto the LORD your God; mourn not, nor**

> **weep. For all the people wept when they heard the words of the law.**
> **10 Then he said unto them, Go your way, eat the fat, and drink the sweet, and send portions unto them for whom nothing is prepared: the joy of the LORD is your strength.**
>
> **—Nehemiah 8**

As the people who had determined to restore the glory of Jerusalem studied the Word of God, they discovered that they were obligated to observe the Feast of Tabernacles.

> **14 And they found written in the law which the LORD had commanded by Moses, that the children of Israel should dwell in booths in the feast of the seventh month:**
> **15 And that they should publish and proclaim in all their cities, and in Jerusalem, saying, Go forth unto the mount, and fetch olive branches, and pine branches, and myrtle branches, and palm branches, and branches of thick trees, to make booths, as *it is* written.**
> **16 So the people went forth, and brought *them*, and made themselves booths, every one upon the roof of his house, and in their courts, and in the courts of the house of God, and in the street of the water gate, and in the street of the gate of Ephraim.**
> **17 And all the congregation of them that were come again out of the captivity made booths, and sat under the booths: for since the days of Jeshua the son of Nun unto that day had not the children of Israel done so. And there was very great gladness.**
>
> **—Nehemiah 8**

(Remember that the Feast of Tabernacles had never once been celebrated under Moses, but rather under Joshua. The reason was that Tabernacles can be celebrated only in the land of promise where there are the necessary trees; never in the wilderness. Something to meditate upon!)

> **18 Also day by day, from the first day unto the last day, he read in the book of the law of God. And they kept the feast seven days; and on the eighth day *was* a solemn assembly, according unto the manner.**
>
> **—Nehemiah 8**

During the time of Jesus on earth it was a custom for the Jews to come in procession to the Temple carrying torches.

The combined light from the processional torches and the candlesticks of the Temple lit up the entire area in and around the Temple.

To the Israelites, who were familiar with this custom, Jesus taught:

> **14 "Ye are the light of the world. A city that is set on an hill cannot be hid. . . .**
>
> **16 "Let your light so shine before men, that they may see your good works, and glorify your Father which is in heaven. . . ."**
>
> **—Matthew 5**

When one studies the traditions which have accumulated around the Jewish celebrations, of which the lights of the Feast of Tabernacles are a beautiful example, one can see the guiding influence of the Holy Spirit. It is a blessed thought to realize that the Jews are so close to the truth of Christ that when God opens their eyes they will move into the worship of God through Jesus Christ in such power and glory that Jerusalem truly will be the joy of the whole earth.

Let us never forget, however, that the inheritance of the saints is available today—right now—to whoever will move ahead in faith and grasp the fullness of God in Christ. The inheritance is open to all—Jew and Gentile, male and female, young and old.

Now is the accepted time. *Today* is the day of salvation.

We can observe the connection between rain (the outpouring of the Holy Spirit) and the celebration of the Feast of Tabernacles (the abiding Presence of God in Christ in the believers), in the following passage from Zechariah 14:

> **17 And it shall be, *that* whoso will not come up of *all* the families of the earth unto Jerusalem to worship the King, the LORD of hosts, even upon them shall be no rain.**

Since the Feast of Tabernacles is the *seventh* convocation, is in the *seventh* month, and lasts *seven* days—a trinity of sevens, we are led to believe that it typifies the consummation and perfection of redemption.

The fulfillment of Tabernacles is the "mark" toward which

Paul was pressing. Tabernacles speaks of our rest in Christ in God, and is associated with the resurrection from the dead, when we are clothed upon with our house from Heaven.

The glorious fulfillment of the Feast of Tabernacles in the Kingdom of God was illuminated clearly in the mind of Christ when He stood and cried:

> **37 . . . "If any man thirst, let him come unto me, and drink.**
> **38 "He that believeth on me, as the scripture hath said, out of**
> **his belly shall flow rivers of living water."**
> **39 (But this spake he of the Spirit, which they that believe on**
> **him should receive: for the Holy Ghost was not yet *given;* because**
> **that Jesus was not yet glorified.)**
>
> **—John 7**

The fulfillment of the Feast of Tabernacles is described in the Book of Revelation:

> **2 And I John saw the holy city, new Jerusalem, coming down**
> **from God out of heaven, prepared as a bride adorned for her husband.**
> **3 And I heard a great voice out of heaven saying, Behold, the**
> **tabernacle of God *is* with men, and he will dwell with them, and**
> **they shall be his people, and God himself shall be with them, *and be***
> **their God.**
> **4 And God shall wipe away all tears from their eyes; and there**
> **shall be no more death, neither sorrow, nor crying, neither shall**
> **there be any more pain: for the former things are passed away.**
>
> **—Revelation 21**

PART II

THE FEAST OF TABERNACLES AND THE CHRISTIAN

9

The Concept of the House of God

During the observance of the Feast of Tabernacles, the Israelites lived outside of their homes in booths constructed from the branches of trees. They were dwelling with God, so to speak. Each year they were to make a special effort to leave the customary pursuits of life for a week, and to spend time meditating upon what the Lord meant to them and had done for them.

The central issue of the Scriptures is that of God abiding in us and we in God. The Kingdom of God is God in Christ in us, and we in Christ in God. This mutual abiding is the basic concept of the new Jerusalem—the Tabernacle of God among men.

When we are perfectly at rest in Jesus Christ, and Jesus Christ is perfectly at rest in us, we have attained perfection.

But let us always keep in mind that it is the rest of God!—it is His rest which is important, not our rest.

It is God's house, the Father's house, which is being constructed.

We who are rooms in God's house benefit immeasurably, it is true. But the fact is, God is seeking a dwelling place for Himself, a living temple constructed from living stones. The house is for God!

When the fulfillment of Tabernacles has come to maturity in our lives, we will be at rest in Christ in God. But—more importantly—God Himself will be enlarged and at rest.

The true Christian saint is occupied primarily with pleasing God, with performing *His* will. Whether the saint's pleasure and will are attained is secondary in importance.

8 And let them make me a sanctuary; that I may dwell among them.

—Exodus 25

13 For the LORD hath chosen Zion; he hath desired *it* for his habitation.
14 This *is* my rest for ever: here will I dwell; for I have desired it.

—Psalms 132

23 Jesus answered and said unto him, "If a man love me, he will keep my words: and my Father will love him, and we will come unto him, and make our abode with him. . . ."

—John 14

49 Heaven *is* my throne, and earth *is* my footstool: what house will ye build me? saith the Lord: or what *is* the place of my rest?

—Acts 7

22 In whom ye also are builded together for an inhabitation of God through the Spirit.

—Ephesians 2

3 And I heard a great voice out of heaven saying, Behold, the tabernacle of God *is* with men, and he will dwell with them, and they shall be his people, and God himself shall be with them, *and be* their God.

—Revelation 21

THE FIRST THREE VISITATIONS

God's point of view is understandable to us in terms of human experience. He desires to rule, bless, and live with people—to be a merciful and gracious King and Father to His children. The accomplishment of God's desire is not as easy as it might seem.

God lived as a neighbor with Adam and Eve in the garden. This was not successful because Adam and Eve did the one thing that God told them not to do. The result was panic on Adam's part and judgment on God's part.

God came down in majesty upon Mount Sinai. But the holiness of God was outraged by the behavior of the people, and the children of Israel were terrified by the awful thunderings and smokings. Such a commotion does not lead to the loving obedience which God is seeking.

God walked among men in Jesus Christ, His Son. But the guardians of the Jewish faith would have none of it. Christ told them plainly that He is the God of their fathers. They laughed in His face, spat upon Him, yanked the hair from His beard.

Finally they crucified Him—the thundering God of Sinai. Again, not an acceptable basis for ruling, blessing, and living with people.

THE TEMPLE OF GOD

Eden! Sinai! Galilee! There was little success from the standpoint of Him Who desires to be a merciful and gracious King and Father to His children. There is another way, and this way will be successful. God is creating a great temple for Himself, of which the Lord Jesus Christ is the chief corner stone, and of which we also are living stones and pillars (Revelation 3:12). That temple is Christ—Head and Body.

The Temple of God is being fashioned now from the personalities of the saints as Christ is being formed in us. By dwelling in Christ, including the great redeemed Body of Christ, God can rule, bless, and live with people. He can be the merciful and gracious King and Father that He wants to be to the peoples of the earth, after He has brought the Church into perfect oneness with Himself in Christ.

As soon as God has perfected the union of the Church with Christ, just as Christ is in perfect union with the Father, then the nations of the earth can be blessed of God and brought into fruitful relationship with Himself (Genesis 22:18, Isaiah 60:5, John 17:21-23, Romans 8:19, Revelation 21:24). God then will be able to rule and dwell among earth's peoples in a manner which will neither permit His own perfect holiness to be violated nor terrify His subjects and neighbors.

The fact that the nations of the earth will be subdued under the rule of Christ as soon as the saints have been brought into complete union with Him does not mean that we are to stop preaching the Gospel to the ends of the earth in the present hour. The Gospel must be preached as a witness to every man, woman, boy, and girl upon the earth—especially in these days when the greatest revival in the history of Gospel power is just breaking upon us.

Nevertheless it is the "Ark of the Covenant," the "Tabernacle of David," to speak symbolically, which is being formed now. The "firstfruits" unto the Lord must be perfected. The ministries and gifts given to the members of the Body of Christ are for the perfecting of the saints until we come to the full stature of Christ (Ephesians 4:12–16).

All the glory, joy, and responsibility—the very best which God has to offer—is available in these days to each and every person, young or old, who will go all the way with the Lord Jesus Christ in sincere, wholehearted discipleship.

After thinking about the self-directed acts of God from the creation of Adam to the coming down of the new Jerusalem, it appears to us that the Scriptures are not as much a record of man seeking God as they are a record of God, out of His own desire and wisdom, building a temple and setting up a kingdom.

As we meditate upon the lives of Adam, Noah, Abraham, Joseph, Moses, David, we can see that the burden of the action was upon God. These men were not perfect, as we usually think of perfection, and they made many human mistakes. But God revealed Himself through them for His own glory. In keeping with this observation, we must realize that the Temple of God tends to be God-centered rather than man-centered.

CHRIST IN YOU

The concept of Messiah dwelling in the members of His Church is one of the major doctrines of the New Testament writings. The forming of Christ in His Body has been the plan of God from the beginning. But it was not until after Jesus' death and resurrection, and the descent of the Holy Spirit, that the mysterious purpose of God became understandable to people.

It may be noticed that we sometimes change the word *Christ,* an Anglicized Greek term, into *Messiah,* its Hebrew equivalent. *Christ, Messiah,* and *Anointed One* are synonyms. The first is Greek, the second is Hebrew, and the third is English. We use these terms interchangeably in order to stimulate thinking.

Most Christians know of the hope of the Jewish people that Messiah will come and deliver them from their troubles, and restore the glory of the kingdoms of David and Solomon. What the Christian Church slowly is coming to understand is that Messiah, the Anointed Deliverer from God Who is going to exalt Israel and establish the Kingdom of God in the earth, consists not only of the mighty Head, Jesus Christ, but also of a mighty Body which now is being formed from each member of the Christian Church who will follow Christ in faithful discipleship.

We say a "mighty" body, not because of any false spirit of exaltation, but because the Body of Christ is part of and is being fashioned from the Divine Substance of the Head, Jesus Christ. It is not that we are anything at all, but that He is working in us (Hebrews 2:11).

The mystery of the Gospel is that Messiah is *in* us. He will appear *to* the world as the visible Christ of the Divine throne of glory. Every eye shall see Him.

And while the members of the Church certainly will behold Him upon the throne of glory, nevertheless the relationship of Christ to His Church is of a much different nature than is true of the relationship of Christ to the world. Christ is being created *in* us. As He is being created in us, the Father and the Son can come through the Holy Spirit and dwell in us forever.

We are not in darkness, as the world is, but even now are experiencing victory as the Lord Jesus Christ brings every enemy in us under His feet. The light of the Day of the Lord is rising within us so that we are not in darkness but are aware of the Presence and purposes of God in Christ.

We are not, of course, confusing our personal reign of Christ and personal day of the Lord, now being experienced by the overcoming Christian, with the historical Millennium and historical Day of the Lord which are yet ahead of us.

The Father's House

It is interesting to note that Stephen's exhortation and testimony (Acts, Chapter 7) proceeded without interruption until he came to the idea concerning the place where God intends to dwell. At this point (Acts 7:49) the Holy Spirit of God assumed control and rebuked the members of the Jewish Council. They were rebuked for resisting the Holy Spirit, for being "stiffnecked and uncircumcised in heart and ears," for betraying and murdering the Lord Jesus.

Notice that the Spirit of God came forth as soon as Stephen began to talk about the finding of a "tabernacle for the God of Jacob." No doubt the reason for the action by the Holy Spirit at this particular point was that the building of the house of God is one of the main burdens of the new covenant. The Father in Christ through the Holy Spirit desires to settle down to rest in the heart of each Christian disciple.

The saints are going to be formed into the Temple of God, the eternal throne of God Almighty, the new Jerusalem. The members of the Jewish Council were under the impression that the important "house," as far as God was concerned, was the Temple of Herod in Jerusalem. Therefore they crucified Jesus because He did not fit into the religious politics which were part of the Temple.

The Council members were rebuked by the Holy Spirit for their hardness of heart and unwillingness to abide in harmony with the will of the Spirit of God.

The Gospel of John contains many comments by Jesus stating that the Father lives in Him, speaks in Him, works through Him.

> **10 "Believest thou not that I am in the Father, and the Father in me? the words that I speak unto you I speak not of myself: but the Father that dwelleth in me, he doeth the works. . . ."**
>
> **—John 14**

Jesus is the Temple of God and God dwells and rests in Him. John 14:2, however, informs us that there are many dwellings in the Father's house. The Temple of God consists of many dwelling units, many abiding places. The Father and the Son desire to find Their rest in a great multitude of hearts, each of which has been fashioned into a holy of holies from which the glory of God can shine forth.

Each Christian is being fashioned as a room in the Body of Christ. Christ, Head and Body, is the Temple of God, the Father's eternal house. It does not matter at all whether we find ourselves in a cottage or a mansion, in Heaven or upon the earth, just as long as God in Christ has found rest in us and we have found rest in Him.

As God has His dwelling in Jesus, in like manner Christ and God want to have Their dwelling in us: living in us, speaking in us, working through us, resting in us. This is the mystery of the Gospel of the Kingdom of God (John 6:56, 57; John 14:23; Colossians 1:27).

The Design

There are two main parts to the concept of Christ being in us. The first part is the entire re-creation of the Christian's personality—spirit, soul, and body (II Corinthians 5:17). The second part is the coming of the Persons of Christ and the Father to dwell in the re-created personality (John 14:23).

Obviously the first part is essential to the second part, since God and His Christ cannot find rest and pleasure in a self-willed, unholy personality (Ephesians 3:16-19; 4:24).

This, then, is the design. God dwells in Jesus Christ. In the same manner, Jesus dwells in us. Since God is in Jesus, and Jesus is in us, then both God and Jesus are dwelling in us. The Scripture states this fact plainly.

Such is the climax of the Christian discipline, a plan and goal far greater than the human mind, worthy of God Almighty, and worked out altogether in and through God's everlasting love toward us.

The Process

Christ in you is the goal toward which the Christian discipleship leads, and also is the means by which that goal is attained. Jesus is the Way to the truth and the life as well as Being the Truth and the Life.

Christ in you is a phrase which can be stated simply and

understood easily. It can be understood easily in a general sense, not including all of the intricate details of the manner in which God brings this experience about in the believer's life.

Although we are going to be setting forth a description of some of the factors which go into the creating of Christ in us, nevertheless an understanding of them is not sufficient to enable us to bring about the abiding of Christ in us. It is the Holy Spirit of God Who, like Eliezer of Damascus, brings the Bride to the Son and Heir (Genesis, Chapter 24).

A young Christian starts out joyously on a shining highway, commencing his or her pilgrimage to the land of promise. After a season of happiness and confidence, the new disciple may find himself groping and stumbling through a desolate wilderness.

At this point of trouble and uncertainty, the goal of *Christ in you* may seem far off and unrelated to the numerous and varied burdens which now have to be borne. The joyous Gospel walk has turned into a struggling through a swamp of doubts and frustrations.

If the Christian does not give up and turn back he begins to learn the many, many lessons which God teaches in the wilderness. The path begins to be visible again from time to time. And *Christ in you* develops from a mental concept into a personal experience of Divine Life.

It is not God's intention that the Scriptures be used only as the basis for a confession of doctrinal belief. Rather, the Scriptures are the Divine testimony which can bring us to a personal experience of Christ within us. It is God Who is working in us both to give the desire for, and also to bring about the accomplishment of, His will concerning us (Philippians 2:13).

Christ in us is the fullness of resurrection life and glory. The power of the Father brings us from Egypt, which symbolizes the bondage to the world, to Satan, and to our carnal nature, all the way to the land of Canaan, which typifies the complete redemption of our spirit, soul, and body; the full indwelling of the Presence of the Father, Son, and Holy Spirit; and spiritual rulership over the material creation. Canaan is resurrection ground!

Notice that the goal of our Christian pilgrimage is not Heaven, although Heaven most assuredly is a real place. Rather, the goal of our journey is the fullness of Christ. The Presence and knowledge of Christ are created within us as the Holy Spirit leads us into areas with which He is familiar but we are unfamiliar.

We are moving toward eternal participation and residence in the holy city, the new Jerusalem, the tabernacle of God among men. We are pressing toward the experience of the Fullness of the Presence of the Godhead. We must fasten our eyes upon the true goal of the Christian discipleship, which is the possession of Christ. "O, that I may know Him!" Paul cried.

It is as though Christ at first were *with* the believer and then, after a season of travail, appears *in* him (John 16:12–22). The natural strength of the believer has begun to be broken and the Life of Christ in him is playing a role of ever-increasing importance in determining his deeds, words, and thoughts (Galatians 2:20).

Although Christ at this hour is preparing His triumphant appearance and entry into the earth followed by His armies, exactly as described in the second chapter of Joel, the third chapter of Habakkuk, and the nineteenth chapter of Revelation, He is also, in the days in which we are living, being formed *in* His saints. The day star, the forerunner of the great Day of the Lord, now is arising in the heart of each disciple who by his godly life and hope of salvation is hastening the Day of Christ.

As faith is increasing in the saints, Christ is being formed in their hearts. As Christ is being formed in their hearts, faith is increasing more and more. "But we all, with open face beholding as in a glass the glory of the Lord, are changed into the same image from glory to glory even as by the Spirit of the Lord" (II Corinthians 3:18).

The process of forming Christ within the disciple is complicated, and there are many different experiences along the way. In the Scriptures God has provided a number of illustrations and doctrines to help us progress successfully through the transition from natural life to spiritual life (I Corinthians 15:45, 46).

The Holy Spirit helps us understand the process of change and the background activities: that is, the rebellion of spirits and their eternal judgment; the resistance maintained by Satan; and the immediate availability of the Presence, power, and authority of the Lord Jesus Christ to every one who asks and is willing to receive. We learn to live in and through the precious body and blood of Christ Jesus.

CHRIST, THE TEMPLE OF GOD

The plan of God from the beginning has been to construct a living temple for Himself. This temple is to be a group of sons of God and brothers of the Lord Jesus Christ (Romans 8:29); a bride for the Lord Jesus (Ephesians 5:32); a weapon in God's hand for the destruction of His enemies (Jude 14, 15); and an eternal dwelling place from which God can contemplate, rule, and enjoy His creation (Psalms 68:18). Here is God's resting place forever (Psalms 132: 13, 14).

The Temple of God is Christ, Head and Body. The Lord Jesus is the great Head of the anointed company. He is the tested corner stone of the building, the elder brother, the first-born from the dead, that in all things He might have the pre-eminence.

The remainder of the structure is being constructed from us Christians. We are the Body of Christ, the fullness of Him Who fills all in all (Ephesians 1:23). Christ, Head and Body, is the Tabernacle of David, Mount Zion, the "hill" where God will dwell forever (Hebrews 12:22). The Christian Church is the new Jerusalem, the Bride, the Lamb's Wife (Revelation 21:2, 3, 9, 10).

To the peoples of the earth, the Temple of God will be Emmanuel—"God with us." The nations will recognize that the Christians are the "seed which the Lord hath blessed" (Isaiah 61:9, John 17:23, Revelation 21:24). The saints will be kings and priests and will reign with Christ throughout the ages of ages (Revelation 22:5).

Some of the passages of Isaiah refer to the effect upon the nations of the earth when the Temple of God has been completed (Chapters 60 and 61, for example). Mount Zion will be the eternal source of Divine light upon the earth.

During the first three days of creation, before God created the sun, moon, and stars, the light of the world came directly from God. As soon as the city of God has been established in the earth, once again the light of the world will come directly from God. But this time it will shine through the Church, which is the Body of Him Who is the Light of the world.

In these days, people will be able to come to the Presence of God who will be dwelling manifestly in the Church. They who come will receive justice, wisdom, healing—whatever they need.

The second chapter of Isaiah gives voice to the burden concerning the Temple of God:

> **2 And it shall come to pass in the last days, *that* the mountain of the LORD'S house shall be established in the top of the mountains, and shall be exalted above the hills; and all nations shall flow unto it.**
>
> **—Isaiah 2**

The preceding passage means that the Christian Church will be the ruling government in the earth. Christ will be the King of kings and Lord of lords. The peoples of the earth will bring their treasures to Mount Zion, the Body of Christ, just as the ambassadors of the nations carried gifts to the court of King Solomon. God has promised Jesus the nations for His inheritance and the uttermost parts of the earth for His possession.

We are joint heirs with Him!

> **3 And many people shall go and say, Come ye, and let us go up to the mountain of the LORD, to the house of the God of Jacob; and he will teach us of his ways, and we will walk in his paths: for out of Zion shall go forth the law, and the word of the LORD from Jerusalem.**
>
> **—Isaiah 2**

It is true even today that only in the Christian Church can the peoples of the earth hear the Word of the Lord. In the days ahead, the world will come to acknowledge its need for the priesthood and the rulership ("the law, and the word of the Lord") of the Body of Christ.

Jesus prayed to the Father for the creation of His Body (John 17:21-26). If there were no other Scripture reference to the eternal house of God we would know, nevertheless, that it will arise in majesty, block upon block, because of the moving of the mighty hand of God through the all-powerful prayers of the beloved Son.

The thought of the glorious days of God's rulership through His Church is inspiring to us. But when we observe the divisions and weaknesses of the Body of Christ we may ask with God, "Can these bones live?" (Ezekiel 37:3).

But then we can rejoice with God because of the certainty that these bones shall live indeed and that they shall stand upon their feet, "an exceeding great army" (Ezekiel 37:10).

When the sons of God are revealed and the full Presence of God in Christ is manifested in them and through them, God and Satan will be facing each other in the earth in a showdown which can have only one outcome. Sin will be judged and the Millennium will commence. This is how the conditions described in the second chapter of Isaiah will be brought about (Romans 8:17-21).

THE RIVER OF LIFE

The Temple of God is described in Ezekiel, Chapters 40 through 48. As is true of many visions of the prophets of the Old Testament, the temple seen by Ezekiel undoubtedly has several meanings. It is likely that the Jews of the captivity would be thinking about the restoration of the Temple of Solomon, whenever a prophet spoke of seeing a temple.

But the scenes which Ezekiel portrayed just before he described the temple, plus some of his statements about the temple which he saw, suggest to us that God may have included some of the spiritual truths which apply to the Body of Christ.

The Body of Christ is the true and eternal dwelling place of God Almighty. Never again will God live in a temple made with hands (Acts 7:48).

Revelation 21:22 states: "And I saw no temple therein: for the Lord God Almighty and the Lamb are the temple of it."

The entire new Jerusalem is the Church, the Wife of the Lamb, the dwelling place of God among people.

Chapter 47 of Ezekiel describes the waters which come out "from under the threshold of the house eastward." This river is the glory of God which is going to be poured out until the whole earth is filled with His brightness and power. "Eastward" points toward the morning of the Day of Christ.

> **21 But *as* truly *as* I live, all the earth shall be filled with the glory of the LORD.**
>
> **—Numbers 14**

> **14 For the earth shall be filled with the knowledge of the glory of the LORD, as the waters cover the sea.**
>
> **—Habakkuk 2**

In symbolic language, Ezekiel 47:9 portrays the outpouring of God's glory which is to stream forth from the members of the Body of Christ:

> **9 And it shall come to pass, *that* every thing that liveth, which moveth, whithersoever the rivers shall come, shall live: and there shall be a very great multitude of fish, because these waters shall come thither: for they shall be healed; and every thing shall live whither the river cometh.**

Notice also verse 12 of the same chapter, and compare it with verses 1 and 2 of the twenty-second chapter of the Book of Revelation:

> **12 And by the river upon the bank thereof, on this side and on that side, shall grow all trees for meat, whose leaf shall not fade, neither shall the fruit thereof be consumed: it shall bring forth new fruit according to his months, because their waters they issued out of the sanctuary: and the fruit thereof shall be for meat, and the leaf thereof for medicine.**
>
> **—Ezekiel 47**

> **1 And he shewed me a pure river of water of life, clear as crystal, proceeding out of the throne of God and of the Lamb.**
>
> **2 In the midst of the street of it, and on either side of the river,**

> **_was there_ the tree of life, which bare twelve _manner of_ fruits, _and_ yielded her fruit every month: and the leaves of the tree _were_ for the healing of the nations.**
>
> **—Revelation 22**

Now, think about John 7:38:

> **"He that believeth on me, as the scripture hath said, out of his belly shall flow rivers of living water."**

The throne of God is the heart of the saint. It is out from the believers, as Jesus has declared, that the rivers of living water are going to flow. In the days in which we are living, Ezekiel's "river" is beginning to flow as Christians are allowing the Holy Spirit of God to show forth the glory of Christ in them.

But in the hour to come, the glory of God in Christ is going to roll forth from the believers until the whole earth is filled with His glory. The Godhead will come and abide in the Body of Christ in far greater power and revelation of Divine glory than was experienced by Israel in the days of the Law of Moses.

> **9 The glory of this latter house shall be greater than of the former, saith the LORD of hosts: and in this place will I give peace, saith the LORD of hosts.**
>
> **—Haggai 2**

There have occurred many marvelous revelations of the Holy Spirit to the Israel of God from the time of Abraham. But the vast floodgates of Heaven are going to be opened in the last days, the time of the return to earth of the Lord Jesus Christ with His saints and holy angels.

> **18 And it shall come to pass in that day, _that_ the mountains shall drop down new wine, and the hills shall flow with milk, and all the rivers of Judah shall flow with waters, and a fountain shall come forth of the house of the LORD, and shall water the valley of Shittim.**
>
> **—Joel 3**

> **11 For as the earth bringeth forth her bud, and as the garden causeth the things that are sown in it to spring forth; so the LORD**

GOD will cause righteousness and praise to spring forth before all the nations.

—Isaiah 61

John 17:22: "And the glory which thou gavest me I have given them" (raising the dead, casting out devils, healing the sick, speaking the words of the Father, the Presence of God, the Holy Spirit without measure); "that they may be one, even as we are one: . . ."

The glory of Christ, which is the life, light, and power of the age to come (Hebrews 6:5), will, according to these words of Jesus in John 17:22, cause the Church to become united in the perfect unity which exists in the Godhead.

Notice how Psalms 133 relates the unity of the brothers with the holy anointing oil which was poured upon Aaron, the high priest.

1 BEHOLD, how good and how pleasant *it is* for brethren to dwell together in unity!

2 *It is* like the precious ointment upon the head, that ran down upon the beard, *even* Aaron's beard: that went down to the skirts of his garments;

3 As the dew of Hermon, *and as the dew* that descended upon the mountains of Zion: for there the LORD commanded the blessing, *even* life for evermore.

Christ, Head and Body, is God's High Priest. The holy anointing oil of the Holy Spirit coming down upon the Body of Christ creates the oneness which is true of the Godhead.

Notice also, in Isaiah 60:5, that the rising of the Lord upon His people, and the putting of His glory upon them, causes them to "flow together":

5 Then thou shalt see, and flow together, and thine heart shall fear, and be enlarged; because the abundance of the sea shall be converted unto thee, the forces of the Gentiles shall come unto thee.

It is a fact that when the disciples are in one accord and the glory of God is abiding upon them, believers by the multitudes are added to the Church (Acts 2:1, 2; 43–47).

The glory of God in Christ is the life-giving water which pours out from under the threshold of Ezekiel's temple. The extent to which the Holy Spirit flows out to the world is related to the degree of unity which God has created among the believers, and to the amount of glory which God has given to them.

As true unity in Christ increases, the glory of God increases; and as the glory of God increases, true unity in Christ increases. An increase in one brings about an increase in the other.

As the unity and the glory increase, the Son of God, Christ Jesus, is revealed to the world, and God is glorified in Him. God has glorified His Son in order that His Son may glorify God.

God has glorified His name once in Christ, and He is going to glorify it again (John 12:28; 17:1). The first glorification was in Jesus Christ, the Head. The second glorification will take place as the authority and power of the Head are revealed in the Body. The best is yet to come. He has kept the good wine until now. The greater works are at hand.

The new Jerusalem is described in the twenty-first and twenty-second chapters of the Book of Revelation. Chapter 22, verse 1, tells of the River of Life. The Church descends from Heaven, having the glory of God (Revelation 21:11). The city of Jerusalem has become the Lamb's Wife, the dwelling place of God among people (Revelation 21:2, 3).

There is no temple in the new Jerusalem because the city itself is the eternal Tabernacle of God. God has taken up His eternal abode in and with His saints and they will be in Him and with Him, and He in them, unto the ages of ages.

From the viewpoint of the rest of the world, the new Jerusalem is the place where God lives and where the nations can come and pay tribute to God Almighty (Revelation 21:24).

God's Temple for evermore is Christ—Head and Body. The overcomers are pillars in that temple and will never again depart from the fullness of His glory—never, never again!

The entire area is "holiness unto the Lord" (Joel 3:17, Zechariah 8:3). Mount Zion has been established in the earth, and God and His Christ have come to live here forever (Ezekiel 37: 26–28). The River of Life, which always is "full of water," is available to all who will drink. The Tree of Life, which is Jesus Christ, and those who are part of Him, provides food and healing for the nations of the earth.

10

The Glory of God—In His House

17 Therefore if any man *be* in Christ, *he is* a new creature: old things are passed away; behold, all things are become new.
18 And all things *are* of God, . . .

—II Corinthians 5

It is a *new* creation. It is the Body of Christ, the eternal habitation of the fullness of the Father and the fullness of the Son through the fullness of the Holy Spirit.

As Christ gains in stature within us we taste the good Word of God and the works of power of the age to come (from Hebrews 6:5). There is in us a healthy appetite for the Word of God; and the saying, "Man shall not live by bread alone" takes on vital meaning to us. There is a deeply-felt hunger for the Bread from Heaven (John 6:48–53). The old things are passing away. All things are becoming new.

TRANSFORMED BY THE GLORY OF THE LORD

The glory of God, which even now is working in the personality of each of us as we give over our lives to the Holy Spirit's guidance and enabling power, is going to increase day by day until we are totally filled and clothed with the Spirit. If we move on with God until the Holy Spirit has become the Source of our life, then, at the coming of our Lord Jesus Christ, the Holy Spirit will make alive our mortal body.

18 But we all, with open face beholding as in a glass the glory of the Lord, are changed into the same image from glory to glory, *even* as by the Spirit of the Lord.

—II Corinthians 3

The text of the third chapter of II Corinthians includes a reference to the face of Moses (verse 13). The condition referred to is described in the thirty-fourth chapter of Exodus:

> **33 And *till* Moses had done speaking with them, he put a veil on his face.**
> **34 But when Moses went in before the LORD to speak with him, he took the veil off, until he came out. And he came out, and spake unto the children of Israel *that* which he was commanded.**
> **35 And the children of Israel saw the face of Moses, that the skin of Moses' face shone: and Moses put the veil upon his face again, until he went in to speak with him.**
>
> **—Exodus 34**

Moses' face was transformed permanently because of repeated exposure to the glory of the Lord. In the same manner the character and personality of the Christian undergo a permanent transformation as he beholds the glory of the Lord in the new covenant.

When we rest our faith upon Jesus Christ the light of the glory of God shines in our heart. Repeated exposure to the glory of God as it is reflected in the face of Christ transforms the disciple, just as the face of Moses was transformed. The overcomer beholds God until he is in God's image and is able to commune with God directly, as was true of Moses.

Therefore Revelation 22:4 is able to announce that "they shall see his face." But Exodus 33:20 declares, "You can not see my face: for there shall no man see me, and live." Anyone who has set his heart upon beholding God will be brought to the death of his sinful and self-centered nature.

> **11 For we which live are alway delivered unto death for Jesus' sake, that the life also of Jesus might be made manifest in our mortal flesh.**
>
> **—II Corinthians 4**

And again:

> **16 For which cause we faint not; but though our outward man perish, yet the inward *man* is renewed day by day.**
>
> **—II Corinthians 4**

The formation of Christ in the heart is not completed instantly (although we are saved from wrath instantly). It is wrought over a period of time while being forged in the fires of temptation, confusion and trouble. It is "precept upon precept, precept upon precept; line upon line, line upon line; here a little, and there a little" (from Isaiah 28:10).

The end result of the Divine transformation is Christian character—character which has been changed permanently into the image of Christ. I John 3:2 declares that "when he shall appear we shall be like him; for we shall see him as he is." We shall have been "changed into the same image from glory to glory, even as by the Spirit of the Lord" (II Corinthians 3:18).

THE IMAGE OF CHRIST

When the Word of God is brought to maturity in our life we will be in the image of Jesus Christ.

> **29 For whom he did foreknow, he also did predestinate *to be* conformed to the image of his Son, that he might be the firstborn among many brethren.**
>
> **—Romans 8**

Our transformation into the image of Jesus Christ is the purpose of God. In line with this purpose we were foreknown, predestined, called, justified and glorified (Romans 8:30). It is interesting to note that the purpose of God, that for which we have been predestined, is not to be born again, or healed, or to exercise our ministry, or even to go to heaven. Rather, the purpose of God is that we be conformed to the image of His dear Son, Jesus Christ.

We need to give more attention to the idea of conformity to the image of Christ because such transformation is of first importance in the mind of God and gives direction to His efforts. Transformation into His image is the "good" for which all things are working—working on the behalf of those who love God, those who are the called according to the Divine purpose (Romans 8:28).

There are at least three areas which must be considered when we set forth the image and likeness of Jesus Christ: (1) His character—what He Himself is in essence, disposition and moral conduct; (2) His relationship with God—He is the eternal habitation of the fullness of the Father through the fullness of the Holy Spirit; and (3) His outward appearance—a human form fashioned from the Substance of Divine Life.

The image and likeness of Christ consists of what He is in character, His relationship to God, and His outward appearance. His soul, spirit and body are in perfect harmony, each making its contribution to the threefold image and likeness. Every single member of the Church, the Body of Christ, will be made perfect in each of these three dimensions. Then, and only then, will the holy city, the new Jerusalem, be ready to descend from heaven upon the new earth (Revelation 21:2).

To be "conformed to the image of his Son" is to have our soul, spirit and body transformed according to the three aspects of Jesus Christ. First of all, His character must be wrought in us. His character consists of what He is in essence, His disposition, and His moral conduct. Our natural life is transmuted into His Essence, which is Divinity, as we partake of His body and blood, and as the Word of God grows within us.

Our disposition is changed as the Holy Spirit instructs us, through the ministries of the Body of Christ and through the circumstances of our daily living, how God expects us to behave. The Spirit teaches us to be gentle, cheerful in adversity, patient in frustrating circumstances, steadfast and reliable concerning our responsibilities, loving and forgiving toward those among whom we dwell, and resolute concerning the will of God.

Our moral conduct is purified as we lay hold upon the authority of the blood of Christ and the power of the Holy Spirit. We completely overthrow and demolish the uncleanness in our behavior. God forgives us and keeps on enabling us to put to death the deeds of our body.

In the second place, we are to become the eternal habitation of the fullness of the Father in the fullness of Jesus Christ through the fullness of the Holy Spirit (John 14:23; John 17: 21-23; Ephesians 2:21, 22; Revelation 3:12). Thirdly, we are going to receive and possess forever a body which is like that of Jesus Christ in form and fashioned from eternal life (Philippians 3:21; II Corinthians 5:4; I Corinthians 15: 53, 54; John 3:16).

Another way of describing the image of Jesus Christ, that

which we are to become, is found in Ezekiel 1:10 and Revelation 4:7. The image and likeness of Christ is pictured as the lion, the ox, the man and the eagle.

The lion is the unconquerable majesty and might of the Son of God. The ox is the ability and willingness of Christ to continue patiently under the heavy load of service to God. The man is the perfected soul, spirit and body of the person—that with which God can have fellowship. God cannot have fellowship with lions, oxen or eagles, only with people who are like Him. The eagle is that ever-renewed resurrection life which soars up from the earth and ascends into the heights of worship and glory.

If we are deficient as the lion, God will add unto us the courage and ability with which to rend and tear the enemies of God. If we are deficient as the ox, God will develop in us the willingness, strength and patience to carry heavy loads over a period of time, as the Lord directs. If we are deficient as the man, God will build us up in soul, spirit and body according to His standards for personal characteristics. If we are deficient as the eagle, God will create "wings" in us so that we can soar into the heavens in the fierce independence and freedom of the sons of God.

The diagram below is one way of displaying the elements which are involved as the saint is brought from total alienation from God all the way to the image of Christ. The making of an atonement, in the fullest meaning of the term, includes this entire transition.

JUSTIFIED	*SANCTIFIED*	*GLORIFIED*
The Word of God in general and specific application	Resurrecting of the disciple	The character of Jesus Christ
The body and blood of Christ	Building up of Christ in the disciple	Filled with the Godhead
The Holy Spirit as the Enabler	Cleansing of the disciple	Clothed upon with a body of eternal life

It can be noticed in this diagram that justification leads to sanctification, and that sanctification leads to glorification. Glorification begins with the developing of the character of Jesus Christ in us.

The maturing of the character of Jesus Christ in us leads to our being filled with all the fullness of God. Our being filled with all the fullness of God leads to our being clothed upon with a body of eternal life.

The grace of God justifies us and leads us into sanctification. The grace of God consists of three elements: (1) the Word of God in general and specific application; (2) the body and blood of Christ; and (3) the Holy Spirit as the Enabler. These three portions of Divinity constitute the grace of God toward us.

The Word of God applied to us generally in the Bible and specifically by personal revelation, the body and blood of Christ, and the Holy Spirit as our wisdom and strength—each has a part to play in the resurrecting of the disciple; in the building up of Christ in the disciple; and in the cleansing of the disciple. It can be seen that each of the three factors of justification creates each of the three factors of sanctification.

The grace of God in justification brings us to sanctification. Being sanctified means that we have been resurrected, that Christ has been formed within us, and that we have been cleansed from the guilt and power of sin.

By the expression "have been resurrected" we are not referring primarily to the making alive of the mortal body at the coming of Christ. Rather, we are speaking of the resurrection life which is being developed in us at this time as we give ourselves over to His death, as the Holy Spirit leads us, and as we begin to experience the power of His resurrection (II Corinthians 4:11, Philippians 3:10).

The three aspects of sanctification—resurrection life, Christ formed within, and moral cleanliness (Aaron's rod, the pot of manna, and the Ten Commandments inside the Ark of the Covenant, to speak figuratively)—create the character of Christ within us. The character of Christ consists of His Divine Substance, His disposition, and His moral conduct.

The Divine Substance of Christ Himself is created within

us and our natural, soulish life is changed into Divine Life, as the Word of God grows within us; as we partake of the body and blood of Christ; as we behold His glory in the ministries and gifts of the Holy Spirit; and as our natural man is brought down to the death of the cross through means of the many experiences which the Holy Spirit brings our way.

The disposition of Christ, that is, the love, joy, peace, longsuffering, gentleness, goodness, faith, meekness, temperance which characterize our Lord Jesus Christ, is the fruit of the Holy Spirit. A disposition such as this can be found in us only as we abide in the life of the Holy Spirit of God; as the Divine Substance of Christ Himself is being created within us; and as we are cleansed of our sin.

The moral conduct of Christ has to do with His absolute obedience to the Father, with His cleaving to the holy ways of the Father, with His love of righteousness, and with His hatred of iniquity. The same type of moral conduct is being created within each believer. We must be forgiven, cleansed and delivered through means of the blood of the cross and through the power of the Holy Spirit. We have to have the very Substance of Christ formed within us if we are to be conformed to the moral conduct of Christ.

We are studying how the Word of God comes to maturity in us. We have mentioned that there are three aspects of the maturing of the Word of God, the maturity of the Word being the image and likeness of Jesus Christ. The three aspects are as follows: (1) the character of Jesus Christ; (2) our becoming the Temple of God; and (3) our being clothed upon with a body of eternal life.

Our discussion then was directed toward the first of these three aspects—the character of Christ. The character of Christ includes His Divine Essence, His attributes of personality which we have termed His disposition, and His moral conduct. To develop the character of Christ in us requires the Word of God, the body and blood of Christ, and the Holy Spirit.

The Word, the body and blood of Christ, and the Holy Spirit are the grace of God. They have been given to us freely and cannot be added to by our fleshly efforts. Because of the precious blood of Christ we have been totally justified in God's sight, having been made free from all condemnation so that we might follow the Holy Spirit all the way to the fullness of the image of Christ.

11

The Building of the Temple of God

There are two parts to our being made the Temple of God. The first part is that of our own personal preparation for receiving the fullness of the indwelling of God. The second part is that of our becoming a part of the great corporate Temple of God, the holy city, the new Jerusalem.

The corporate Temple of God will be assembled from individual "stones," each of which has been made perfect in advance. There will be no imperfect unit in the Temple of God. God is taking exceedingly great care with each stone at this time so that when the building comes together it will be perfect.

4 *He is* the Rock, his work *is* perfect: . . .

—Deuteronomy 32

10 For we are his workmanship, created in Christ Jesus unto good works, which God hath before ordained that we should walk in them.

—Ephesians 2

The Temple of Solomon is a type of the corporate Temple of God. The stones were not shaped on site as they were being placed in the structure. Rather they were prepared in advance before they were hauled to the building site. They had been formed so expertly that there was no sound of hammering while the Temple of Solomon was being erected. This extraordinary accomplishment was possible only because of the careful planning, skill and effort which went into the stones prior to their being assembled into the Temple.

7 And the house, when it was in building, was built of stone made ready before it was brought thither: so that there was neither hammer nor axe *nor* any tool of iron heard in the house, while it was in building.

—I Kings 6

Years of preparation preceded the construction of Solomon's Temple. Before David died he gave to Solomon the plans for the Temple (I Chronicles 28:11–19). Also, David collected much of the material that was used in the Temple (I Chronicles 28:2–9), particularly precious metals and stones. Solomon, in his God-given wisdom, carried forward the work of preparation by contracting with Hiram, the King of Tyre, for cedar and fir lumber. In addition, Solomon obtained the stone blocks for the foundation of the Temple.

> **17 And the king commanded, and they brought great stones, costly stones, *and* hewed stones, to lay the foundation of the house.**
> **18 And Solomon's builders and Hiram's builders did hew *them*, and the stonesquarers: so they prepared timber and stones to build the house.**
>
> **—I Kings 5**

So it is with the eternal Temple of God. God Almighty is the designer and builder of it. Only eternity will reveal the amount of thought, time and material which God has spent, is spending, and will yet spend upon His holy dwelling place. It is a living temple, for the Temple of God is Christ—Head and Body.

There is no resource in the universe which will be withheld if its contribution is needed. In fact, "all things work together for good to them that love God, to them who are the called according to his purpose." And His purpose is that we might be joined together with His beloved Son, the Lord Jesus Christ, and become one with Christ in God.

We, as individuals, must be fashioned into the image of Christ. If we are not in the image of Christ, God will not be able to find His rest in us (Psalms 68:18). All of the ministries of the Body of Christ work to the end that we might be created in the image of Christ and that Christ might be brought to the fullness in us (Ephesians 4:7–13).

God will dwell only in Christ, and the more of Christ we have the more of God we will be able to receive. Each one of us must allow God to finish, to perfect His work in us no matter how pleasant or unpleasant the process may become. For only as we become perfect in His sight will we be ready to be fitted into the corporate Temple of God which shall rule over all of God's creation unto the ages of ages (Revelation 22:5).

The Temple of God will be composed of each individual who has been made ready in advance through means of the Word of God, through means of the body and blood of Christ, and through means of the Holy Spirit. We must lay hold upon the grace of God which has been freely given to us, so that God's grace can fashion us into a perfect fit in the Temple.

In the mind of God there is an exact spot in His Temple for each one of us. There is a position in the structure which each of us as an individual can fill. God knows that exact place and what will be required of that part throughout eternity. He has foreknowledge, and we have been predestined according to that foreknowledge (Romans 8:29).

It is possible for any one of us to miss out on God's best by not attending to the things of God as we should. But God will see to it that the construction of the Temple goes ahead on schedule. Someone else will take our place. Therefore, we behave wisely when we strive for God's highest and best plan for our life.

> **11 "Behold, I come quickly: hold that fast which thou hast, that no man take thy crown.**
>
> **12 "Him that overcometh will I make a pillar in the temple of my God, and he shall go no more out: and I will write upon him the name of my God, and the name of the city of my God, *which is* new Jerusalem, which cometh down out of heaven from my God: and *I will write upon him* my new name. . . ."**
>
> **—Revelation 3**

It is clear, then, that since God will dwell only in Christ we must have Christ formed in us if we expect God to take up His abode in us. Having the promise of becoming a temple of God (II Corinthians 6:16), we must "come out from among them, and be ye separate, saith the Lord, and touch not the unclean thing" (II Corinthians 6:17). We have to "cleanse ourselves from all filthiness of the flesh and spirit, perfecting holiness in the fear of God" (II Corinthians 7:1)

If we keep on laying hold upon the Lord Jesus Christ each day of our Christian life, and do not quit because of unbelief or because of some trial or temptation, we finally will be ready to be placed into our assigned location in the great Temple of God. There is a certain place in the Temple of God which has been reserved for each saint.

> 2 "In my Father's house are many mansions: if *it were* not *so*, I would have told you, I go to prepare a place for you. . . ."
>
> —John 14

> 20 And are built upon the foundation of the apostles and prophets, Jesus Christ himself being the chief corner *stone;*
> 21 In whom all the building fitly framed together groweth unto an holy temple in the Lord:
> 22 In whom ye also are builded together for an habitation of God through the Spirit.
>
> —Ephesians 2

The preceding passage from Ephesians reminds us of God's declared intention to have an eternal dwelling place, as set forth in Exodus 25:8:

> 8 And let them make me a sanctuary; that I may dwell among them.

The whole Body of Messiah, the Temple of God, is built up by means of the gifts and ministries of all the Christian people.

> 15 But speaking the truth in love, may grow up into him in all things, which is the head, *even* Christ:
> 16 From whom the whole body fitly joined together and compacted by that which every joint supplieth, according to the effectual working in the measure of every part, maketh increase of the body unto the edifying of itself in love.
>
> —Ephesians 4

Peter speaks of the "lively stones":

> 5 Ye also, as lively stones, are built up a spiritual house, an holy priesthood, to offer up spiritual sacrifices, acceptable to God by Jesus Christ.
>
> —I Peter 2

12

One In Christ In God

The change in our personality of which we have been speaking up to this point might be termed the maturing of the born-again experience. We have referred also to the indwelling of the fullness of God; but our main point of emphasis has been upon the change in us in preparation for our being indwelt by the Lord.

We have talked about the power of the blood of Christ to make atonement, the initial spiritual resurrection of the believer, the planting of the Word of God in our heart, bringing our daily conduct under the discipline of the Holy Spirit, the growth of the Word of God in us, putting to death the deeds of our body, and the maturing of the Word of God in us. Through the processes of God in redemption we are becoming a "new creation" (II Corinthians 5:17).

But all of the above are changes in us—our personal transformation of spirit, soul and body. The coming of the Persons of the Godhead to abide in us is yet another matter. God comes into us at the moment of our receiving Christ. But He desires to come to us in a much greater way as soon as we have been made ready for Him.

The new covenant is the creating of the image of Christ in the mind and heart of the believer (Hebrews 8:10). It is an inner work. Christ *in* us is the hope of glory. As the likeness of Christ begins to appear in our inner being the glory of God can begin to take up residence in us to an increasingly greater extent. Peter admonishes us to take heed to the Scripture until the day of the Lord dawns within us.

> **19 We have also a more sure word of prophecy; whereunto ye do well that ye take heed, as unto a light that shineth in a dark place, until the day dawn, and the day star arise in your hearts:**
>
> **—II Peter 1**

The Lord Jesus told us the very same thing:

> **23 Jesus answered and said unto him, "If a man love me, he will keep my words: and my Father will love him, and we will come unto him, and make our abode with him. . . ."**
>
> **—John 14**

After we receive Christ we are to study the Scriptures, both Old and New Testaments. As the Holy Spirit makes clear to us the directives and the promises, we are to look to the Spirit for the wisdom and strength to do the will of God. We make use of every help which the Lord has given us, including the Bible, prayer, assembling with fervent believers, the communion service and so forth. We practice diligently the good works set before us, such as giving, working in the local church, receiving and operating the gifts of the Spirit, and assisting the work of Christ wherever and whenever possible. We *do* the will of God, by His help, thus "building our house upon the rock."

As we take heed to the things of Christ a wonderful transformation occurs within us. Christ is formed in us. As Christ is formed in us the Father and the Son come to dwell within us. They make their abode with us.

Our task is to keep the words of Jesus and to open the door of our heart to Him.

> **20 "Behold, I stand at the door, and knock: if any man hear my voice, and open the door, I will come in to him, and will sup with him, and he with me. . . ."**
>
> **—Revelation 3**

God's plan is described in Ephesians 3:14–19:

> **14 For this cause I bow my knees unto the Father of our Lord Jesus Christ,**
>
> **15 Of whom the whole family in heaven and earth is named,**
>
> **16 That he would grant you, according to the riches of his glory, to be strengthened with might by his Spirit in the inner man;**
>
> **17 That Christ may dwell in your hearts by faith; that ye, being rooted and grounded in love,**
>
> **18 May be able to comprehend with all saints what *is* the breadth, and length, and depth, and height;**
>
> **19 And to know the love of Christ, which passeth knowledge, that ye might be filled with all the fulness of God.**

Before the Father and the Son can take up residence within us we must be strengthened in the inner man. We must be converted in the depths of our character, not just in our mind.

The prayer of Paul for the saints at Ephesus was that they might be "strengthened with might by his Spirit in the inner man." He prayed that Christ might dwell in their hearts by faith—the faith which comes as a result of the strengthening of the inner man by the Spirit of God.

The increase of Christ in the heart means an increase in our possession of the love of Christ. Being established in the love of Christ makes it possible for the saint to begin to grasp the extent of God's glory. As we begin to grasp the extent of the glory of God we grow closer to the place where we can be filled with all the fullness of God. We become the eternal dwelling place of the Godhead. God finds His rest in us. We find our rest in God.

The Father dwells in Christ in totality.

9 For in him dwelleth all the fulness of the Godhead bodily.

—Colossians 2

The Father loves the Son and dwells in Him completely. All that the Father is and possesses He has given to the Son. The Father is in the Son in His fullness and the Son is in the Father in His fullness. If we can understand the relationship of the Son to the Father, then we can gain some understanding of the relationship of the Body of Christ to the Son.

21 "That they all may be one; as thou, Father, *art* in me, and I in thee, that they also may be one in us: that the world may believe that thou hast sent me. . . ."

—John 17

Jesus prayed for the filling of the saints with the fullness of the Father and the Son. The prayer is recorded in John, Chapter 17.

"That they all may be one";

Although various denominations have come into being over the last several hundred years, the Body of Christ, the Temple of God, is one. Its division into sects is superficial. At one call from the Lord the members of the Body of Christ will flow together in perfect unity.

"as thou, Father, art in me, and I in thee,"

The unity of the Body of Christ is a spiritual unity which comes about through means of the impartation of the Substance of God.

The Christian Church is much more than groups of saved people. The Church is born from above; "not of blood, nor of the will of the flesh, nor of the will of man, but of God" (John 1:13). The Body of Christ, the Temple of God, is, in fact, the Substance of Christ which has been imparted to men through the Holy Spirit.

Eve was Adam in another form, having been fashioned from Adam's rib. She was not created of the dust of the ground, but from a piece of Adam. In like manner the true and only Christian Church is not made from flesh and blood. It is the Substance of Christ, taken from Him and formed within people. That true Church, which is Christ in another form, always and forever abides in absolute unity because it is all created from the one Christ of God. The Body of Christ is one with the unity which exists only in the Godhead.

"that they also may be one in us":

It is not that the Church is *one* which is so significant. It is that the Church is one in the Father, Son and Holy Spirit. Being one *in the Godhead* makes all the difference in the world. If the Christian Church became one apart from the Godhead it would be the greatest enemy of Christ in the universe. It would be the worst antichrist of all time.

"that the world may believe that thou hast sent me."

The churches are attempting in their own strength, to a great extent, to influence the world for good; and certainly there are many worthy works of all kinds going on. But God's revival is yet ahead of us. Once the Body of Christ, the Temple of God, has been brought to perfection through the ministries of the Holy Spirit (Ephesians 4), then, and only then, will the Body be filled with all the fullness of the Godhead.

And when the Church becomes one with the Father and the Son, then the world will believe that the Father indeed did send the Son. The world will never believe that God sent Christ until the Church becomes one in the Godhead.

"And the glory which thou gavest me I have given them";

The Father imparted to the Son the fullness of His own glory. Christ has passed on to us the fullness of the glory of God. We do not as yet have the fullness of the glory of God because we are not able to receive it. But the Holy Spirit is making us ready to receive the glory of God, if we are moving along under His direction.

If we are not moving along in the Holy Spirit, but are idly standing by without seeking to grasp more of Christ, then we are not being made ready to receive the glory of God. There are no limits placed upon the glory of God given to the Son by the Father. There are no limits placed upon the glory of God given to the Church by the Son.

"that they may be one, even as we are one":

The Body of Christ will be absolutely perfect in unity. It is "one tabernacle" (Exodus 26:6). There will be not so much as a shadow of disunity in the Body. The unity of the Body of Christ is being created by the Lord God. The Body will be one in the glory and in the love of God. The perfected unity of the finished Body of Christ can be compared only to the unity which exists in the Father and the Son.

"I in them, and thou in me,"

God the Father dwells totally in God the Son. The Son will dwell totally in His Body. Therefore the Body of Christ has the totality of God because the Father is in the Son.

The Father will dwell only in Christ. He who has Christ has the Father also. He who has the fullness of Christ has the fullness of the Father. He who does not have Christ does not have any part at all in the Father because the Father dwells only in the Son. The more of the Son we have the more of the Father we have as a result. The Father is pleased to dwell in the Son because He loves the Son and has given all things into His hands.

"that they may be made perfect in one";

Each member of the Body of Christ will be made perfect. If there were one imperfect member, the Body would be imperfect. In addition, the Body has a perfection in its completeness which is not true of an individual member.

In the Body of Christ, as is the case also with the human body, the whole is greater than the sum of its parts. The finished Body of Christ is the new Jerusalem, and it has a perfectness of design which makes it a completely adequate instrument for the residence of the Lord God and for the blessing of the nations of the earth.

We cannot make ourselves perfect in these terms of perfection. Our task is to be absolutely obedient to the Holy Spirit. We are learning daily how to be obedient as the Spirit brings us through the appropriate experiences. The Spirit's assignment is to bring each one of us to the perfection which Christ has ordained for us, for which He prayed in John 17, and which is necessary for the end He has in mind. The Holy Spirit accomplishes this perfection by many methods, including the use of the ministries and gifts which He alone gives and empowers.

"and that the world may know that thou hast sent me,"

Today the world is confused about the Person of Christ. There appears to be general consent that He was a good man, probably a philosopher who died in order to demonstrate the sincerity of his beliefs.

The soldiers who guarded Christ and who stood around the base of the cross were typical of the people of the world: some mocked; some gambled for His clothing; some offered Him vinegar to drink; one "glorified God, saying, Certainly this was a righteous man" (Luke 23:47).

There is no agreement on the part of the world regarding the man, Christ Jesus. In the meanwhile, the Church is on its way to maturity, attempting to preach the good news to every creature while it itself is growing in grace.

But once the Church has reached maturity and has been made one in the Godhead, the world will know that God Almighty sent Jesus Christ. There will be no confusion, no uncertainty. Then the world of its own choice will go to the Church for instruction in righteousness (Isaiah 2:3).

"and hast loved them, as thou hast loved me."

There is no limit to the love of God for the Church. God loves the Son, and God loves the Bride of the Son with that same love. Notice in the context of the above passage, that God loves the Church when Christ is in it—when it has been made perfect in the Father and the Son. If God so loved the world while yet in its sinful state that He was willing to give His only begotten Son for its redemption, how much more does God love the Church which the Holy Spirit has fashioned from the body and blood of God's dear Son?

There still is a great deal of our personality which is hostile toward God. He therefore waits patiently while Christ works in the garden of our life, rooting out all that is displeasing to God and nourishing the new Plant which now is growing there.

The unhindered love of God abides upon the Church because the Church has been born of Christ. The Church is loved with the same love with which the Father loves the Son.

When the world sees the glory of the Father and the Son abiding upon a Church which is completely one with the Father and the Son, then the world will know that the Father loves the Church with the same love with which He loves the Son.

> **24 "Father, I will that they also, whom thou hast given me, be with me where I am; that they may behold my glory, which thou hast given me: for thou lovedst me before the foundation of the world. . . ."**
>
> **—John 17**

Although it may be difficult for us to understand, and it may appear to conflict with our independence of thought and action (it does not conflict in actuality), the members of the Body of Christ were given to the Son by the Father. It is not a case of our choosing Christ, though from our point of view it seems that we did it all ourselves. The truth of the matter is, however, that the Father brings us to Christ.

We are a called-out people, just as Israel of old. The Lord adds to the Church daily such as should be saved. Every member of the Body of Christ is a gift of the Father to the Son; and when we come to Christ He does not cast us out (John 6:37). No man can come to Christ unless the Father draw him (John 6:44). If we are to understand the true quality of the Church and the attitude of the Father toward the Church, then we must realize that every member of the Church is hand-picked and presented to Christ by the Father.

"be with me where I am";

Christ is upon the highest throne of the universe. He is at the right hand of God Almighty. There is no greater throne. Christ has all authority in heaven and upon the earth. He is exalted to a point past the ability of the mind of man to conceive. Yet, He has summoned us to this level. How can that be? It is the unfathomable love of Christ for His Bride which so commands.

"that they may behold my glory,"

When we speak of the glory of Christ we have only a faint notion of what we are describing. The glory of Christ is so all-consuming that the mightiest of the angels in the highest level of heaven draw back in reverent fear whenever Christ is exercised. The communication between the Father and the Son is so wrapped in Divine fire that none of the heavenly host can bear to witness the exchange. It is the glory which upholds the stars in their courses, billions of which are larger than our sun.

The glory of Christ is absolutely unimaginable and unapproachable in its staggering extent. It cannot be described by the language of men. His Presence and authority fill all things and extend into infinity and eternity. He created all things and can destroy all things just as easily and quickly.

"which thou hast given me":

The Father has given His glory to Christ. But since the Father and Christ are in perfect unity the glory remains with the Father. When the Church reaches maturity, then it can become one with Christ and the Father and receive the fullness of the glory of God. God will not give His glory to another. Therefore we must become one with Him in order to receive His glory.

"for thou lovedst me before the foundation of the world."

We do not know much about Jesus Christ as He was before the world was founded. We do know that "all things were made by him; and without Him was not anything made that was made" (John 1:3). It appears that the "Lord" of the Old Testament in many instances, or perhaps in every instance, was Christ and that it was His Spirit Who spoke in the prophets of Israel (I Peter 1:11).

Christ was before Abraham. He spoke the worlds into existence. He was the Word in the beginning. He was with God and was God. Before the world was founded the Father loved the Son.

Then there came into the mind of the Father a concept of the perfect Church, the Bride and Body of Christ. God proceeded to set in motion the forces which would in time bring a perfect "wife" for the Word, a wife who herself would be the Word—in His image in every detail. Everything which has happened since that time has been for the purpose of bringing forth the wife of the Word. All of this has come about because of the love of the Father for the Son.

In the Book of Revelation the Bride is not called the wife of the Word, nor is she called the wife of the Son of God, nor even the wife of Christ. She is called the "Lamb's wife" (Revelation 21:9). It is the "marriage of the Lamb" which is going to come (Revelation 19:7).

The reason for this terminology is as follows: the Church is created upon the Substance of Christ which was taken from Him. The Church eats His body and drinks His precious blood. His body was broken for us and His blood was shed for our sins. It was the Lamb of God Who was slain for us and Whose body was broken and the blood shed. Therefore, the Church is married to the Passover Lamb.

Because we live by eating His flesh and drinking His blood we are united to Him in Substance. We are united, or married, to the Lamb Whom God gave for our protection, for our cleansing, and for our transformation into life (John 6:54).

"O righteous Father, the world hath not known thee":

The world has sought God in many different ways, from the lustful rites of savages to the more refined but no more effective philosophies of scholars. But God cannot be found through the efforts of the flesh any more than an ant can master algebra. It is utterly impossible for the unregenerate human being to lay hold upon God in his own strength.

The world does not know God and is attempting at the present time to construct a social order apart from God. God laughs in derision at the preposterous spectacle of the dust of the ground attempting to thrust aside the power which formed it. All of the efforts of mankind to do anything at all without God end in disaster for all concerned.

God Almighty is God indeed, and He chooses the time, place and manner of imparting the knowledge of Himself to the proud flesh of the earth. In His great love He has given to us His Son as an offering for our sins. The gift of Calvary is a perfect gift, entirely worthy of God. Whoever will humble himself as a child can have the free gift of God. But whoever attempts to meet God on some basis other than Calvary is traveling down the wrong road. The end is total destruction. We must come God's way, or else perish.

"but I have known thee, and these have known that thou hast sent me."

We of the Church know beyond all doubt that Christ came from God. Therefore we put all of our faith, trust and hope in Him. We know that all of the Substance of God is in Christ and that He alone has the authority and power to present us to the Father. Christ is the door to God and there is no other way.

26 "And I have declared unto them thy name, and will declare *it:* that the love wherewith thou hast loved me may be in them, and I in them."

—John 17

"When the Lord shall build up Zion, he shall appear in his glory" (Psalms 102:16). We are being built up in Christ in order that we may be able to receive the love with which the Father loves the Son, and may be able to receive the fullness of Christ. The ministries and gifts of the Holy Spirit, as well as our environment and circumstances, are all working together to bring us into conformity to the image of Christ.

As soon as we have been completed He will appear upon the mount of transfiguration, so to speak. We will appear with Him in glory and the world will be convinced that Christ was sent from the Almighty God of the universe, and that God loves the Church with the same love with which He loves His Son.

We must be made ready in the meantime, and learn the lessons to be gained from each circumstance in which God places us. People are conformed to the image of Christ in the situation where they are, just as the blocks of Solomon's Temple were fashioned at the quarry. God's workmen are exceedingly skillful, and in the Spirit's time the Temple of God will be erected with no forcing being necessary.

When we hear the sound of "hammering" (the sound of a believer being worked into shape by various situations in which the Holy Spirit places him or her) we know that the blocks are still at the quarry. God is supervising intently the forming of each block in accordance with the specifications of His master plan. At the precise moment the "blocks" of the Temple of God will "flow together" (Isaiah 60:5) and the world will know that God has constructed His holy dwelling place. No man can assemble the stones of the Temple of God. We can, however, pray to the end that Jerusalem will be made a praise in the earth.

> **1 FOR Zion's sake will I not hold my peace, and for Jerusalem's sake I will not rest, until the righteousness thereof go forth as brightness, and the salvation thereof as a lamp *that* burneth.**
>
> **—Isaiah 62**

When Solomon's Temple was assembled it was filled with the glory of God.

> **10 And it came to pass, when the priests were come out of the holy *place*, that the cloud filled the house of the LORD,**
>
> **11 So that the priests could not stand to minister because of the cloud: for the glory of the LORD had filled the house of the LORD.**
>
> **—I Kings 8**

In God's house there are many dwelling places (John 14:2). If Jesus were to be the only dwelling place of God, He would have told us. But there are going to be a multitude of "homes" in the great house of God. Jesus went away in order to make ready a place for us. He is going to return for us in order that we may be with Him where He is.

It is His will that each one of us become a home, a room, in the Temple of God. Our being joined with Christ in the love of God brings great pleasure to God and Christ, and it is to this end that God has planned and operated all things in the world.

> 16 Know ye not that ye are the temple of God, and *that* the Spirit of God dwelleth in you?
>
> —I Corinthians 3

> 16 And what agreement hath the temple of God with idols? for ye are the temple of the living God; as God hath said, I will dwell in them, and walk in *them;* and I will be their God, and they shall be my people.
>
> —II Corinthians 6

13

An Eternal Weight of Glory

1 FOR we know that if our earthly house of *this* tabernacle were dissolved, we have a building of God, an house not made with hands, eternal in the heavens.

—II Corinthians 5

Here we see our two bodies in contrast. Our present physical body is liable, as was Paul's, to dissolution. Paul was in danger of his life on many occasions, the most recent instance having occurred "in Asia" (II Corinthians 1:8). None of us knows when our body may succumb to sickness or to an accident. But we have also a "building of God, an house not made with hands, eternal in the heavens." That house cannot be dissolved. The "weight" of that house has to do with our "light affliction." Our present body will be glorified by being clothed upon with that eternal body.

2 For in this we groan, earnestly desiring to be clothed upon with our house which is from heaven:

—II Corinthians 5

From Paul's writings we know that he was pressing toward the "mark" of the clothing over with the house from heaven. Once we get past Pentecost in our Christian experience the Holy Spirit begins to create within our hearts the fervent desire to press on to the attaining of the body of resurrection life.

Of course, we always are more than willing to escape this present wilderness, whether by death, by translation, or by any other means. But such a desire is to be expected when one compares the life of bliss which God's creatures enjoy in Paradise with out daily problems in the world. Who wouldn't want to go to heaven? And yet, there are loved ones in this world, and these ties of love temper our desire to go home to be with the Lord Jesus.

But the clothing over with the body of life—that is something else again! That is no sorrowful leaving of loved ones upon the earth so that we can go to Paradise. Rather, the clothing over with life is the triumphant overcoming of the last enemy. That is victory! That is joy! That is reunion!

On that Day there will be no breaking hearts (among those who have served the Lord faithfully), no tears of anguish then. For that is the Year of Jubilee, when the slaves go free and everyone returns to his inheritance in the Lord. May God hasten the day when the sons of God are revealed!

The Spirit of Christ in Isaiah portrays the exceeding joy and glory of the saint at the moment of being clothed upon with eternal life:

> **10 I will greatly rejoice in the LORD, my soul shall be joyful in my God; for he hath clothed me with the garments of salvation, he hath covered me with the robe of righteousness, as a bridegroom decketh *himself* with ornaments, and as a bride adorneth *herself* with her jewels.**
>
> **—Isaiah 61**

We already have the first installment (earnest) of the Holy Spirit. But if we serve Christ faithfully until He comes, or until we go home to be with the Lord, whichever comes first, then we can look forward to that Day when our mortal body is made alive by His Spirit Who dwells in us (Romans 8:11). The same Spirit Who raised Christ from the dead will set our body free through His eternal power and glory.

> **3 If so be that being clothed we shall not be found naked.**
>
> **—II Corinthians 5**

It appears from the Scripture that some Christians will be saved apart from any reward. They will be saved in that Day but will be found naked as far as any spiritual accomplishment is concerned.

> **15 If any man's work shall be burned, he shall suffer loss: but he himself shall be saved; yet so as by fire.**
>
> **—I Corinthians 3**

It seems certain that some will be saved who have not laid up for themselves an eternal weight of glory. They will not be destroyed in the Day of God's wrath, but they will be found "naked."

The next verse in II Corinthians 5 points up—perhaps more than any other verse in the Bible—the desire of the saints for immortality:

> **4 For we that are in *this* tabernacle do groan, being burdened: not for that we would be unclothed, but clothed upon, that mortality might be swallowed up of life.**
>
> **—II Corinthians 5**

We who are in this body of flesh do groan because we are burdened. But we are not groaning "that we would be unclothed" (leave the body and go to heaven). Rather, we are groaning that we might be clothed upon with resurrection life. We are groaning that "mortality might be swallowed up of life."

Paul asks, "O wretched man that I am! who shall deliver me from the body of this death?" (Romans 7:24).

God's answer to Paul is, "The Lord Jesus is coming with a house not made with hands, eternal in the heavens. The Holy Spirit Who now dwells in you will make alive your mortal body and you will be free from sin and death just as your Lord Jesus Christ is free from sin and death."

Resurrection life is going to swallow up mortality, as portrayed by the covering over of the acacia wood of the Ark of the Covenant with gold (Exodus 25:10, 11).

Acacia wood, symbolizing mortality, was always present in the Ark. But it was never seen because it was completely covered with gold, which typifies Divinity. Our original body will be our dwelling place throughout the ages to come. But it will never be seen as it is now because it is going to be "swallowed up of life."

Jesus still has the same body. He still has the nail prints in His hands. But He is in a greatly glorified state. After we stand in the Presence of God Almighty for a few billion years, steadfastly beholding His Face, we will be so glorified that every atom of our being will be changed into the Divine Nature. However, our original form will be there, just as the outline of the leaf can be traced in the rock after eons have passed.

So, we are not groaning that we might leave our body and fly away, although that indeed is a blessed prospect. Rather, we are longing for and hastening toward the putting on of the "far more exceeding and eternal weight of glory," our "house not made with hands, eternal in the heavens."

Our hearts are overcome with joy as we consider the greatness of the inheritance which is to be ours at the return of the Lord. We yet shall possess the righteousness and peace for which we are fighting in the Lord. We are laboring to enter the rest of God. It will be ours if we do not give up but continue on as one faithful to Him Whose name is "Faithful" (Revelation 19:11).

God is preparing us for the putting on of the house from heaven.

> **5 Now he that hath wrought us for the selfsame thing** [to be swallowed up of life] ***is*** **God, who also hath given unto us the earnest of the Spirit.**
>
> **—II Corinthians 5**

God has created us for the purpose of conforming us to the very image of His only begotten Son, Christ Jesus, in order that He might be the firstborn among many brothers. We must be conformed absolutely to His express image in our spirit, in our soul, and in our body.

It is God's great joy and good pleasure that we inherit His fullness. There is no greater joy to the heart of God than that which comes from beholding His sons fight their way by faith into the fullness of all that He has prepared for them. Israel displeased God in not maintaining the courageous faith required for the full possession of the land of promise. Let us not be like them. Let us rather go on until death itself, that last enemy of our Lord Jesus Christ, has been crushed under our feet by the God of peace (Romans 16:20).

We have the Holy Spirit as an earnest, a guarantee, a pledge, a first installment upon the greater glory which is yet to come. The greater glory will include, among other blessings, the clothing over of our body with a house fashioned from eternal life. Let us never lose sight of that goal for it is the fullness of salvation. The pursuit of the fullness of God is His will for us right now. We need faith and patience if we are to lay hold upon our entire inheritance in Christ Jesus.

We are always confident and willing to leave this fleshly body and to go home to be ever present with our wonderful Lord Jesus. As long as we are at home in the body we are absent from Him. So we labor on in the pursuit of righteousness in order that we may be accepted of Him whether we be present with Him or still in a mortal body.

But beyond all of this is the sure knowledge that we have an eternal house in the heavens, and that we will be clothed upon with it if we keep our gaze steadfast upon Christ. For we must yet appear before the judgment seat of Christ that we may receive the consequences of the way in which we have answered His call upon our life.

> **10 For we must all appear before the judgment seat of Christ; that every one may receive the things *done* in *his* body, according to that he hath done, whether *it be* good or bad.**
>
> **—II Corinthians 5**

The body of resurrection life is a reward for faithfully serving Christ no matter what the inconvenience or pain may be. From the context of the above verse we understand that Paul was thinking about the reward which will come to the Christian who has labored in Christ in order that the will of God might come to pass in the earth. Paul was considering that "far more exceeding and eternal weight of glory" which is to be his at the appearing of the righteous Judge.

After having accepted the free salvation in Christ, a person may or may not go on to the gaining of a reward.

> **14 If any man's work abide which he hath built thereupon, he shall receive a reward.**
>
> **15 If any man's work shall be burned, he shall suffer loss: but he himself shall be saved; yet so as by fire.**
>
> **—I Corinthians 3**

Every one of us will stand before the Judgment Seat of Christ. We will hear Him say, "Well done, good and faithful servant." Or He may be caused to say, "It became necessary for me to remove those things which hindered you, but you remained faithful throughout your fiery trial. Welcome to my kingdom." Christ shall wipe away our tears and we shall be saved from the wrath of God.

We will not come to experience the fullness of life, the authority and power, and the fruitfulness which will be assigned to those who labored more diligently in the Lord. But our cup will run over with blessing, peace and happiness, and we will worship Him forever and ever, world without end.

There seem to be some misconceptions concerning the giving of rewards under the new covenant. Consider, if you will, the following two seemingly inconsistent statements:

> **4 Now to him that worketh is the reward not reckoned of grace, but of debt.**
>
> **Romans 4**

> **12 "And, behold, I come quickly; and my reward *is* with me, to give every man according as his work shall be. . . ."**
>
> **—Revelation 22**

In Romans 4 Paul appears to be saying that if we do nothing at all except believe in Christ, God will reward us in terms of our belief. But if we do anything about our salvation, then God owes us something and this interferes with His grace.

In Revelation 22, however, John informs us that Christ is going to reward men according to their works. These two passages seem to be in opposition. Romans appears to state that there is no reward for good works, but Revelation maintains that there is.

The seeming clash between Paul and John is brought about by the fact that they are referring to two different aspects of salvation. In Romans, Chapter 4, Paul is declaring that the law of Moses is not the way to obtain the righteousness of God.

Paul presents Christ as the answer to our need for right standing with God. If a man "works," that is, if he attempts to gain God's favor by keeping the laws and ordinances of the old covenant, then he is avoiding the cross of Christ.

Through keeping the law of Moses he hopes to earn the reward of God's approval upon his life. Therefore, a righteousness which comes through faith in God's Lamb is not necessary. He has gained the reward through blameless observance of the law and the Levitical ordinances. But God no longer will accept this approach!

Revelation 22:12, on the other hand, is not referring to the strict observance of the Levitical statutes and ordinances as being the "work" which earns the reward from Christ. Rather, the "work" of Revelation is referring to the type of Christian faithfulness of which Christ speaks so highly in Revelation, Chapters 2 and 3.

For example, "I know thy works, and charity, and service, and faith, and thy patience, and thy works; and the last to be more than the first" (Revelation 2:19). The works mentioned here have nothing at all to do with the observance of the Levitical statutes—that to which Paul was referring in Romans 4:4.

Paul is speaking of our reward in II Corinthians 5, and a surpassingly glorious reward at that! Our mortal body is going to be clothed over with a body of resurrection life. We are going to reign with Christ from His very throne, at the right hand of the Almighty (Revelation 3:21). We will inherit the "all things" of Revelation 21:7.

> **27 "For the Son of man shall come in the glory of his Father with his angels; and then he shall reward every man according to his works. . . ."**
>
> **—Matthew 16**

> **14 If any man's work abide which he hath built thereupon, he shall receive a reward.**
>
> **—I Corinthians 3**

> **23 And whatsoever ye do, do *it* heartily, as to the Lord, and not unto men;**
> **24 Knowing that of the Lord ye shall receive the reward of the inheritance: for ye serve the Lord Christ.**
>
> **—Colossians 3**

> **8 Look to yourselves, that we lose not those things which we have wrought, but that we receive a full reward.**
>
> **—II John**

The house from heaven is a reward for uncompromising faithfulness to the Lord Jesus Christ. It is the crown of incorruptible righteousness, glory and life.

25 And every man that striveth for the mastery is temperate in all things. Now they do it to obtain a corruptible crown; but we an incorruptible.

—I Corinthians 9

8 Henceforth there is laid up for me a crown of righteousness, which the Lord, the righteous judge, shall give me at that day: and not to me only, but unto all them also that love his appearing.

—II Timothy 4

12 Blessed *is* the man that endureth temptation: for when he is tried, he shall receive the crown of life, which the Lord hath promised to them that love him.

—James 1

4 And when the chief Shepherd shall appear, ye shall receive a crown of glory that fadeth not away.

—I Peter 5

10 ". . . be thou faithful unto death, and I will give thee a crown of life. . . ."

—Revelation 2

It may be noted that Paul's whole life, as we found in Philippians, Chapter 3, was pointed straight as an arrow on a fully-drawn bow. Paul's target was (is) the full knowledge of Christ—the arrival at the resurrection out from among the dead. Paul exhorts us to march along with him and not break rank. "Follow me," he cries, "as I follow Christ." Paul had already been saved. Now he was seeking the full attainment of life! of righteousness! of glory! of fruitfulness! of authority and power! Who will follow Paul as he follows Christ? Will you?

READINESS FOR TRANSLATION

The promise of God is that if we live in the Spirit of God each day of our Christian pilgrimage we finally will come to the time when God delivers our mortal body "from the bondage of corruption into the glorious liberty of the children of God."

Think of it! Our physical body will be made alive througn means of the Holy Spirit Who at this time is dwelling in us. And our body not only will be made alive but also will be filled with love for the things of the Spirit of God, as is true now of our born-again inner nature.

Instead of a desire for adultery there will be a desire for God Himself. Instead of a desire for uncleanness there will be a desire for purity. Instead of a desire for indecent acts there will be a desire for holiness of conduct.

In place of the desire for things and the worship of things will be the desire for God and the things of God. In place of hatred will come love for God and for His people. Witchcraft will be replaced by faith in God's Word; envy, by contentment with our place in God; wrath, by peace; strife, by the wish to better the condition of our brothers and sisters in the Lord.

Instead of drunkenness our resurrected body will seek self-control. In place of the spirit of heaviness will be the garment of praise. Grief and anxiety will be swallowed up by love, joy, power and a sound mind.

Our inner man longs for these changes from sin to righteousness to take place in us right now. And so they do, as we begin to bear the fruit of the Spirit of God. But the mortal flesh in which we are housed has some ideas of its own. It far prefers the original state of affairs. We certainly have to give ourselves wholly to the Spirit of God in order to keep the body in submission, or else the body will take over our thoughts and actions.

The clothing over of our present body with the body from heaven will abolish the bodily tendencies toward sin and will bring us immortality. The main idea of the coming of Christ is not that we will go to heaven, although that surely will occur and the thought of it is enough to cause the heart of the overcomer to take up the fight with renewed vigor. But the meaning of the coming of Christ, as far as the overcoming Christian is concerned, is the being clothed upon with the body from heaven so that complete and perfect righteousness of life is obtained.

We go to heaven, it is true. But the best part of all is that heaven comes to us and fills us with the righteousness and life of heaven. That is salvation! That is redemption! Let us therefore put to death now the uncleanness of the flesh and spirit so that we will be prepared for the change in us which is coming with the appearing of our Lord Jesus Christ with His holy angels.

There are many reasons why a proper preparation must be made now if we are going to be ready for the redemption of our body when Jesus comes. We must, by the Spirit, "put to death the deeds of the body." Without such preparation it is impossible for us to have an abundant entrance into the "everlasting kingdom of our Lord and Savior Jesus Christ" (II Peter 1:11).

First of all, it is not reasonable to suppose that God is going to clothe us with a body like the glorious body with which Jesus is clothed unless and until our spirit and soul have been made ready. If we are weak in the faith, undecided about serving the Lord, doubleminded, unfaithful, then we are not ready to be clothed upon with the power and authority of eternal life. The cherubim are still guarding the tree. The overcomers are the ones who have access to the tree of life (Revelation 2:7).

The body of glory is synonymous with authority and power over the nations—with the throne of Christ. We must be prepared to rule in and with Christ. Our inner man must be prepared and strengthened for the Divine glory which is going to descend upon us. If the fullness of the glory of God were to come upon us at this point we might not be able to bear so much of the presence of God Almighty. Paul prays concerning this:

> **16 That he would grant you, according to the riches of his glory, to be strengthened with might by his Spirit in the inner man;**
>
> **17 That Christ may dwell in your hearts by faith; that ye, being rooted and grounded in love,**
>
> **18 May be able to comprehend with all saints what *is* the breadth, and length, and depth, and height;**
>
> **19 And to know the love of Christ, which passeth knowledge, that ye might be filled with all the fulness of God.**
>
> **—Ephesians 3**

We must be strengthened in the inner man before we will be able to receive the fullness of God. Otherwise, that which is meant for our good might prove to be harmful to us.

Enoch and Elijah were translated into the presence of God, and it seems that this has been true of other saints as well (Matthew 27:52, 53). Do we have enough faith for this experience?

The Scripture teaches us that Enoch was translated "by faith" (Hebrews 11:5). Is our faith strong enough for translation glory? If our faith fails in that day we might look back.

Jesus has warned us about looking back! Remember Lot's wife (Luke 17:32).

The point is that we need to be strengthened in faith now, bearing the fruit of faith in increasing measure, so that when the great trumpet of God sounds we will have the faith required for the receiving of the fullness of God's glory. Faith will be required for a successful response to the mighty summons of Christ in that Day.

Then too, we need to ask if we really desire to live that close to God all the time. Are we really going to enjoy dwelling in such close relationship to the fiery holiness of God Almighty? Is that what we truly want?

> **14 . . . Who among us shall dwell with the devouring fire? who among us shall dwell with everlasting burnings?**
>
> **—Isaiah 33**

Perhaps we need to think twice before we seek to rush into the presence of God in the pursuit of the body of eternal life.

> **2 But who may abide the day of his coming? and who shall stand when he appeareth? for he is like a refiner's fire, and like fullers' soap:**
>
> **—Malachi 3**

The greatest reward prepared for the saint is the nearness to God and the continual beholding of His face.

> **4 And they shall see his face; and his name *shall be* in their foreheads.**
>
> **—Revelation 22**

If our goal in life is to abide in the fullness of the presence of God forever, being clothed in a righteous and immortal body, then we need to begin to purify oureselves through the power of the Holy Spirit. If we do not, then our actions testify that closeness to God is not our goal after all. We are seeking God with the mind and mouth, but not with our heart.

God loves us too much to bring us into a situation where

we would be miserable and where we would make others around us miserable. The atmosphere of heaven is filled with perfect love and harmony. A spirit of gentle good will, of thinking the best about everyone, of meekness and selflessness of attitude, permeates every area of Paradise. Would we bring into Paradise our gossiping, our hating, our murmuring, our criticizing?

Love, peace, joy and complete and perfect obedience to the Father characterize the saints in Glory, the Elders, the elect angels and the other inhabitants of heaven. People who rush about in the violent passions of the body and spirit would not get along well in heaven. God is not going to seal the doom of an immature, self-centered person by clothing him or her with eternal life.

True, the new body will be an aid to righteous living. But the new body alone cannot live a holy life. And being in heaven will not guarantee a loving obedience to God on our part. Satan and his angels originally were in heaven, and it is not recorded that there was a law of sin governing their bodies. Yet they rebelled against God! It is the love for righteousness and hatred of iniquity which is inherent in the Nature of Christ which must govern the spirit and soul of the believer, and his body as well. Righteousness, holiness and obedience are developed within us while we are upon the earth in mortal bodies.

We demonstrate now, in this life, our determination to live the kind of life that is found in heaven and that characterizes the inhabitants of heaven—those with whom we are seeking fellowship. We show our determination by putting to death the deeds of our fleshly body. We reveal on earth whether or not we are citizens of heaven. Living in the flesh works against our being prepared for the heavenly attitude and behavior.

There is this about Enoch, Elijah, Moses and other heroes of faith: they please God. They are the kind of people God and Jesus enjoy having around themselves. David is a man after God's own heart. Moses and Elijah appeared with Jesus as He prayed on the mountain, and they discussed "his decease which he should accomplish at Jerusalem" (Luke 9:31). There is a heavenly fellowship and it is pleasing to the Lord, just as the fellowship of like-minded people is enjoyable to us. If we say that we love God and enjoy His company, and we do not obey God or work with the Spirit in putting to death the deeds of our carnal nature, then there is a question about whether we really love God after all (I John 2:15).

The maturing of Christ within us, which is the same as the maturing of the fruit of the Spirit within us, will create in our personality a heavenly attitude radiating blessings and good will toward all of God's creatures, and terror toward the workers of darkness. If this kind of attitude and actions is being developed within us, then our ruling with Christ over the nations of the earth will bring about the kind of environment for earth's peoples which God desires. There will be a peaceful, happy and righteous spiritual and social environment. Persons who, in Christ, can accomplish such a government will be clothed by the Spirit of God with a body of eternal life and will be invested with Divine authority and power over the earth.

The "dew" of the Holy Spirit upon the grave of a saint is as the natural dew upon a plant—it is going to result in life and growth.

> **19 Thy dead *men* shall live, *together with* my dead body shall they arise. Awake and sing, ye that dwell in dust: for thy dew *is as* the dew of herbs, and the earth shall cast out the dead.**
>
> **—Isaiah 26**

The physical remains of the Spirit-filled Christian have been "sealed" by the Lord. They are not the same as the remains of the sin-filled unbeliever. The anointing of the Holy Spirit, Who abode upon Elisha, remained in his bones after his death.

> **21 And it came to pass, as they were burying a man, that, behold, they spied a band *of men;* and they cast the man into the sepulchre of Elisha: and when the man was let down, and touched the bones of Elisha, he revived, and stood up on his feet.**
>
> **—II Kings 13**

Each one of God's saints who is alive in Christ has the stamp of God upon the members of his mortal body. At the summons of Christ the body of the Christian will respond to the Life of Christ—the mighty Holy Spirit of God. The grave of the believer will open and the Holy Spirit will convert his body into an eternal state.

The parable of the ten virgins (Matthew 25:1-13) is a good illustration of the need for readiness during the Day of the Lord; of the relationship between the quality of our Christian life now and our fitness for the body of life when Jesus comes; and of the necessity for having the anointing of the Holy Spirit upon our life now in order that we may participate in triumph in the resurrection out from among the dead at the appearance of the Lord Jesus Christ.

The virgins took their lamps (the Light of Christ within them) and went forth to meet the bridegroom (started out on their Christian pilgrimage). The virgins who "took no oil with them" represent Christians who live in the flesh rather than in the Spirit of God.

When the bridegroom delayed his coming they all slumbered and slept, speaking of the fact that the Christians of the first century and of succeeding centuries have died without witnessing His expected appearing.

"At midnight there was a cry made," indicating that the glorious appearing of our Lord will take place at "midnight"—at the time of the maturing of sin upon the earth.

"Then all those virgins arose"—the time of the resurrection had come. But the five foolish virgins discovered to their dismay that the light of Christ within them had gone out because they had not obtained enough oil (the anointing of the Holy Spirit). While they set about to seek the Holy Spirit, the five wise virgins went in to the marriage and the foolish virgins were left outside the door.

When we say that the virgins have the anointing of the Holy Spirit we are not referring to speaking in tongues, or any of the gifts of the Spirit, as valuable as these tools are for the building up of the members of the Body of Christ. Rather, we are referring to the anointing which is upon the cross-carrying overcomers who are living and walking in obedience to the Holy Spirit, who are learning to love righteousness and hate iniquity, and who therefore carry the abiding presence of the glory of the Lord in their lives.

So shall it be at the appearing of Christ. Those Christians who have died with the anointing of the Holy Spirit upon their lives will be caught up to meet the Lord, as will those Christians who are alive at that time and who are walking in the Spirit of God. But those Christians who have lived after the flesh, whether they are dead or alive at the coming of Christ, will not have the anointing which will be required in that Day. All of us need more of the abiding presence of the Holy Spirit during every moment of our time and throughout every part of our personality and behavior.

As part of our preparation for ruling with Christ, and for the first resurrection which is associated with our ruling in Christ (Revelation 20:4, 5), we first must suffer. The cross and the crown go together.

> **17 And if children, then heirs; heirs of God, and joint-heirs with Christ; if so be that we suffer with *him*, that we may be also glorified together.**
>
> **—Romans 8**

> **10 "Fear none of those things which thou shalt suffer: behold, the devil shall cast *some* of you into prison, that ye may be tried; and ye shall have tribulation ten days: be thou faithful unto death, and I will give thee a crown of life. . . ."**
>
> **—Revelation 2**

Paul linked knowing the power of Christ's resurrection with knowing the fellowship of Christ's sufferings.

> **10 That I may know him, and the power of his resurrection, and the fellowship of his sufferings, being made conformable unto his death;**
>
> **—Philippians 3**

The Book of First Peter shows us the necessity for our sufferings, and comforts us with the hope of the "glory that shall be revealed."

For example:

> **7 That the trial of your faith, being much more precious than of gold that perisheth, though it be tried with fire, might be found unto praise and honour and glory at the appearing of Jesus Christ:**
>
> **—I Peter 1**

It is through sufferings that we are brought to the place where we can cease from sin and live no longer "in the flesh to the lusts of men, but to the will of God." It is through sufferings that we come to experience the power of resurrection life and thus are prepared for the body fashioned from resurrection life.

Another way in which God views our pursuit of eternal life and glory is as a business transaction. The grace given to us in Christ and the gifts and ministries of the Holy Spirit are pictured as sums of money. We can apply the money in a business-like way, thus earning interest and making a profit. Or we can refrain from using the Divine money, keeping it out of circulation. God is very displeased with the latter action. Lack of diligence in the use of God's money is one way to be caught short when Jesus appears.

> **20 "And so he that had received five talents came and brought other five talents, saying, Lord, thou deliveredst unto me five talents: behold, I have gained beside them five talents more.**
>
> **21 "His lord said unto him, Well done, *thou* good and faithful servant: thou hast been faithful over a few things, I will make thee ruler over many things: enter thou into the joy of thy lord. . . ."**
>
> **—Matthew 25**

The parable of the talents shows us that the Christian who has attended diligently to the gifts of God which have been given to him will take part in the joy of Christ at His appearing. The joy of Christ is the inheriting of the heathen and the possessing of the uttermost parts of the earth. Included also, of course, is the surpassing joy of the fullness of life in the Holy Spirit of God.

But the slothful Christian will not find the Day of the Lord to be such a pleasant experience. A wrathful Lord Jesus will say to him: "Thou wicked and slothful servant, thou knewest that I reap where I sowed not, and gather where I have not strawed: thou oughtest therefore to have put my money to the exchangers, and then at my coming I should have received mine own with usury. Take therefore the talent from him, and give it unto him which hath ten talents. For unto every one that hath shall be given, and he shall have abundance: but from him that hath not shall be taken away even that which he hath.

"And cast ye the unprofitable servant into outer darkness: there shall be weeping and gnashing of teeth" (Matthew 25: 26–30).

The gifts and ministries which God has given to us as an individual may seem small to us now, but Jesus knows that if we are not faithful in the use of them we would not be faithful with greater responsibilities. However, if we faithfully use the gifts which He has given to us, seeking His will in all that we say and do, then we can be trusted with the riches of the Kingdom when Jesus returns.

We know that the coming Day of days will bring redemption to the Body of Christ in that our physical bodies will come forth from the grave and we will live and rule with Jesus Christ forever and ever. Eternal life is the great hope of the Gospel of Christ. If we follow Jesus with all of our strength, and the glory of God rests upon our life, then the sting of death is removed from us and the victory of the grave is turned into defeat (I Corinthians 15:55).

Enoch (Genesis 5:24) and Elijah (II Kings 2:11) are forerunners of those who will be taken up to God at the appearing of Christ. Whether or not Christians are physically alive at His coming is of little consequence (I Thessalonians 4:15). The important factor is that the glory of God must rest upon us if we are to attain to the first resurrection from the dead. It appears that many of the saints arose right after Christ's resurrection and joined with Him in His great triumphal procession (Matthew 27:52, 53) as a sheaf of the firstfruits of the earth (Leviticus 23:10).

When Jesus returns, the great multitude of those who have died in Him will rise to meet Him in the air. It is the bodies of the disciples which will be rising from their place of burial, because the born-again spiritual nature of each believer will be returning from heaven along with the Lord Jesus (I Thessalonians 4:14, Colossians 3:1–4). These are God's saints who have suffered with Christ, who have been faithful unto death, and who now are receiving the crown of righteousness, glory and eternal life.

If we hope to be clothed over with the body of resurrection life, then we must be strengthened in the inner man. Our faith must be brought up to translation strength. We must be purified so that we will enjoy dwelling in the fiery holiness of God's presence. We must adopt the heavenly attitude and behavior.

We must come under the discipline of the Holy Spirit, being quick to confess our sins and to forsake them through means of the wisdom and strength given to us by the Holy Spirit. We must forsake all in order to know Christ, to know the power of His resurrection and the fellowship of His sufferings, being struck down in the likeness of His death in order that we might experience the likeness of His resurrection. We must take up our cross and follow Christ daily, diligently employing our talents in the building up of the Kingdom of God, faithfully carrying out each small task and responsibility.

Therefore, let us not be among those who neglect their salvation. Let us rather be "followers of them who through faith and patience inherit the promises" (Hebrews 6:12).

14

The Kingdom-Wide Fulfillment of The Feast of Tabernacles

Now we come to the kingdom-wide fulfillment of the Feast of Tabernacles. To do so we pass from the Millennial reign of Christ over into the new heaven and earth reign of Christ. The fulfillment of everything that God has purposed concerning all persons and all things reaches completion in the new heaven and earth reign of Christ—that which is described in the twenty-first and twenty-second chapters of Revelation. Therefore, the efforts and events prior to the coming down to the new earth of the glorified Wife of the Lamb have as their focus the bringing to pass of the conditions of the new heaven and earth reign of Jesus Christ.

There are at least six aspects of the new heaven and earth reign of Christ which are foreshadowed in the elements of the Feast of Tabernacles:

1. The completion of the harvest of all crops grown in the land of promise—"Behold, I make all things new";
2. The tabernacling of God with mankind—"Behold, the tabernacle of God is with men";
3. The living waters—"And he showed me a pure river of water of life, clear as crystal, proceeding out of the throne of God and of the Lamb";
4. Eternal service to God—"his servants shall serve him";
5. The law of God—"they shall reign for ever and ever"; and
6. The light of the world—"the Lamb is the light thereof."

To begin with, the Feast of Tabernacles (Leviticus 23:39-43) marks the end of the harvest season. All of the food grown in the land of Israel had by this time been reaped and processed. Beginning with the citrus harvest in February and March and continuing through the wheat, vegetables, corn, figs, grapes, nuts and so forth, all had been gathered and threshed or otherwise prepared by the time of the Feast of Tabernacles. It was a celebration of the most extreme joyfulness and gratitude toward the Lord. God had received His people and had blessed them. The long drought of summer was over and the September (early, former) rains were about to commence.

> **39 Also in the fifteenth day of the seventh month, when ye have gathered in the fruit of the land, ye shall keep a feast unto the LORD seven days: on the first day *shall be* a sabbath, and on the eighth day *shall be* a sabbath.**
>
> **—Leviticus 23**

It is easy to see how the new heaven and earth reign of Christ is associated with the Feast of Tabernacles. Everything which God has planted in the Christian has reached maturity. Christ has come forth in each aspect of the personality. There is nothing whatever left of the first creation.

> **17 Therefore if any man *be* in Chrsit, *he is* a new creature: old things are passed away; behold, all things are become new.**
>
> **—II Corinthians 5**

God demonstrates clearly that the past is over and done by creating a new heaven and a new earth.

> **13 Nevertheless we, according to his promise, look for new heavens and a new earth, wherein dwelleth righteousness.**
>
> **—II Peter 3**

Notice that God creates the new heaven first, then the new earth. God always creates the heaven before the earth. That is the way He works with us Christians. He is creating the "heaven" in us, the spiritual domain, first. After we have a "new heaven," so to speak, He then will create for us a "new earth"—a new body.

The Tabernacles—new heaven and earth—phase of the redemption which is in Christ Jesus marks the completion of the work of redemption and atonement in the believer. The spirit of the Christian has been made one with the Spirit of the Lord (I Corinthians 6:17). His soul, or inner man, has been transformed into pure gold, having been refined in God's fires of suffering and filled with the Nature and Substance of Christ. His mortal body has been made eternally alive by being clothed over with a body from heaven which has been fashioned from the substance of eternal life.

The harvest and process of the personality is now finished, and the long drought of summer is ended. The new year, with its refreshing rains and its hopes and expectations for a future too glorious to imagine, has now arrived.

> **5 And he that sat upon the throne said, Behold, I make all things new. And he said unto me, Write: for these words are true and faithful.**
>
> **—Revelation 21**

The symbolism of the elements and activities of the Feast of Tabernacles suggests to us that the new heaven and earth reign of Christ has to do with the completion of the "harvest of all crops grown in the land of promise," which is a figurative way of saying the maturing of all that God has planted in the personalities of His children.

A second concept which is common to both the Feast of Tabernacles and the new heaven and earth reign of Christ is that of the dwelling of God with mankind. It can be seen that the idea of the tabernacling of God with people is central to all that we are saying to the reader.

TABERNACLES, AND THE HABITATION OF GOD

God finds rest in us and we find rest in God. We abide in God and God abides in us. The main concept which stands out as we think about the new heaven and earth reign of Christ is that of the abiding and resting of God Almighty and the Lamb in the new Jerusalem, the Bride of the Lamb.

During the Feast of Tabernacles the Israelites lived in booths. The Jews were commanded to build little booths of tree branches outside of their houses and to live in them for seven days. The term *tabernacles* (temporary dwellings) is derived from these booths in which the Hebrews dwelled during the celebration.

> **42 Ye shall dwell in booths seven days; all that are Israelites born shall dwell in booths:**
>
> **43 That your generations may know that I made the children of Israel to dwell in booths, when I brought them out of the land of Egypt: I *am* the LORD your God.**
>
> **—Leviticus 23**

Once each year the Israelite family, no matter how rich or poor, was to put together a small booth of palm and willow branches, and other foliage, and live in it for a week under the stars. This change in their routine of living gave them the opportunity to bring to mind their history ("that your generations may know that I made the children of Israel to dwell in booths, when I brought them out of the land of Egypt"); and also to think about their special relationship to God as His chosen people.

Also, the booths pointed toward the day when the people of God become the eternal Tabernacle of God (Revelation 21:3).

Sometimes it becomes necessary for us to take a moment to remember who we are, what we are doing, where we are going, and what our relationship is to God. We continually must call to mind our individual role as a king and priest of God; otherwise we get sidetracked and lose our purpose and direction in all that we are and do. Other interests and desires capture our imagination and heart. God is jealous of these side issues. He desires our complete attention at all times (Exodus 34:14).

During the new heaven and earth reign of Christ the nations of the saved shall pursue their own interests. They "walk in the light" of the Bride of the Lamb and "bring their glory and honor into it" (Revelation 21:24). But the Wife of the Lamb spends eternity in worship of God and in union with His Being. Her role is priestly, and she never for one moment forgets her purpose among the nations of the earth. She cannot lose sight of her service and destiny because God Almighty and the Lamb are tabernacling in her midst.

> **3 And I heard a great voice out of Heaven saying, Behold, the tabernacle of God *is* with men, and he will dwell with them, and they shall be his people, and God himself shall be with them, *and be* their God.**
>
> **—Revelation 21**

The above passage sums up the whole work of God, from the creation of the heaven and the earth all the way to the descending of the new Jerusalem from the new heaven to its eternal resting place upon the new earth.

It has always been God's desire to dwell among His creatures, but sin has made it impossible. From the hour of Adam's sin to the malicious treatment which Jesus received at the hands of the Jewish elders and the Roman soldiers, most people have not been able to do justly, love mercy, and walk humbly with God. It is not possible for us humans to conduct ourselves in this simple and good manner because of our inheritance of sin, our iniquitous "shape" (Psalms 51:5), and the poisonous spiritual atmosphere of the age in which we live.

God revealed His eternal purpose, in Exodus 25:8:

> **8 And let them make me a sanctuary; that I may dwell among them.**

Just thirteen words, but they encompass the Godhead, mankind, heaven, earth and thousands of years of suffering, travail, triumph and glory.

Jesus added to the revelation of God's intention to dwell in people, in John 14:23:

> **23 Jesus answered and said unto him, "If a man love me, he will keep my words: and my Father will love him, and we will come unto him, and make our abode with him. . . ."**

From Jesus we learn that the dwelling place of God is going to be a living temple rather than one made from stone, gold, wood and other nonhuman materials.

Paul enlarged our understanding of the living Temple of God by his teachings concerning the Church, the Body of Christ. It is Christ, Head and Body, Who is the Temple of God.

> **19 Now therefore ye are no more strangers and foreigners, but fellow-citizens with the saints, and of the household of God;**
>
> **20 And are built upon the foundation of the apostles and prophets, Jesus Christ himself being the chief corner *stone;***
>
> **21 In whom all the building fitly framed together groweth unto an holy temple in the Lord:**
>
> **22 In whom ye also are builded together for an habitation of God through the Spirit.**
>
> **—Ephesians 2**

We are being "builded together for an habitation of God through the Spirit." There is no statement in the Bible more central to the workings of the Lord God.

Why then does God not come into the Church in His fullness and take up His residence in us now? Why all the confusion, delay, tribulation, worry, grief of mind and heart, and pain of body?

It is because we cannot dwell with Him in our present condition. The fire of His presence would destroy us. He does not enjoy our ways and we do not enjoy His ways. He loves us and we love Him, but the sin and rebellion remaining in us is at enmity with God.

The Ark of God always must come to rest in a prepared place. Your entire personality must welcome the presence of God. You must be willing to wait upon God's pleasure at every moment and in all circumstances. How many of us attempt to keep Jesus in some inconspicuous place in our life, so that we can use Him when we get ready, and yet not inconvenience ourselves to any great extent?

It may be true that many of us Christians are not quite ready to fully receive the presence of God into our life and thereby give ourselves over wholly to His likes and dislikes, His ways of doing things. It is difficult for two strong-minded people to live in harmony together. Too many cooks spoil the broth! God has definite ideas of His own and He takes no pleasure in having to explain in detail everything He is going to do before we will move, and then have to resist our stubbornness at every turn. We have so very much more to learn! so much more to become!

The eternal habitation of God is the glorified Church, the Body of Christ, the Wife of the Lamb. The twenty-first and twenty-second chapters of the Book of Revelation inform us that gold and precious stones predominate in the construction of the new Jerusalem. The pure transparent gold is the Substance of Christ within us which has been refined in us through sufferings—the only method which accomplishes the desired transparency—until we are as clear as glass (I Peter 1:7).

The assortment of precious stones which embellish the foundations of the wall of the city speak of the different Christian personalities which have been formed through great heat and pressure, under the precise supervision of the Holy Spirit, until their infinitely-varied radiances shine forth. The result of the Holy Spirit being manifested through these separate personalities produces one hue, and then another, in a heavenly rainbow of color.

The gates are pearl, because pearl is created in response to suffering. The "pearl" in our nature is built up layer upon layer, as we patiently bear the cross which has been assigned to us. As God sends us grace to get through the day, another layer is added to our pearl.

The pearl in us is hard material, not easily penetrated because it is formed at the deepest level of consecration—the secret place of the heart of the saint where God and he work out the transformation day by day. Thus the gates which control entrance into the city are of the highest quality pearl. It is only through prolonged patience in tribulation that we become capable—from God's standpoint—of being admitted into the presence of God and of the Lamb.

The new Jerusalem is the eternal resting place of the Ark of God's glorious presence. The city is perfectly proportioned and of immense size, constructed of gold set with precious stones. The light of the Holy Spirit shining through the facets of the jewels fills the new earth with soft, multi-colored light—perhaps many hues never before beheld upon the earth.

This pure light, this beauty, this array of infinitely-varied colors which renders unnecessary the light of the sun and moon, reveals to us that the Bride of the Lamb is perfect—absolutely perfect—in every minute detail. No longer does God have to compromise His deepest wisdom and desires in order to dwell among His children. The Church has been so wrought upon by the Holy Spirit of God that it has become an absolutely fitting dwelling place for the Lord God Almighty and His Son, Jesus Christ.

No adjustment whatever is needed. God is perfectly at home in every square inch of His Temple. As the billions upon untold billions of eternities roll by, the house of God will become increasingly imbued with all that God is until God and His Temple are indivisible, indistinguishable. God will be in His house and His house will be in God to the degree that separation is no longer possible. This is true marriage. Physical marriage on the earth is a type of the true marriage which can exist only between the Lamb and His Wife.

Therefore, the reason for the delay in God coming to us and dwelling in us, in accordance with His eternal purpose in Christ, is that we have not as yet been fully prepared. We are being brought to maturity at this time. No doubt our service to God and mankind throughout the thousand years of the Millennium will result in ever-increasing refinement of our nature because of our close contact with Jesus Christ. One fact is certain—the new Jerusalem does not descend in radiant beauty until *after* the Millennial Jubilee has been completed.

We are being prepared today for the abiding of God in Christ Jesus:

> **16 That he would grant you, according to the riches of his glory, to be strengthened with might by his Spirit in the inner man;**
>
> **17 That Christ may dwell in your hearts by faith; that ye, being rooted and grounded in love,**
>
> **18 May be able to comprehend with all saints what *is* the breadth, and length, and depth, and height;**
>
> **19 And to know the love of Christ, which passeth knowledge, that ye might be filled with all the fulness of God.**
>
> **—Ephesians 3**

God dwells in Christ in His fullness because Jesus is a perfectly prepared place for God. In all of Jesus' ministry upon the earth we see God the Father. Jesus always is perfectly at rest in the Father, and through Him the Father is able to dwell among men.

Every person who sees Jesus sees the Father. Men do not need to ask to see the Father or to inquire what the Father is like. We can see the Father's moral character in Christ. We can behold His works of power in Christ. We can hear His words from Christ. Thus Jesus Christ is the perfect fulfillment of the Levitical Feast of Tabernacles.

The destiny of the Church is the attainment of total rest in God and Christ. The Day will come when mankind will be able to observe God Almighty through Christ in the Church. Men will see the moral character of the Father, behold the works of power of His hands, and hear His words—all through the members of the Body of Christ. The Church will be the revelation of God in Christ, and God will find His rest in Christ—Head and Body.

The Church will come down from the new heaven and remain forever in the new earth. Through the Church, God will be approachable to the peoples of the new earth.

In our time the Body of Christ is the dwelling place among men and manifestation of God in Christ. But our sinful flesh tends to muddy the water of eternal life and to obscure the "light of the knowledge of the glory of God in the face of Jesus Christ" (II Corinthians 4:6).

We who are members of the Body of Christ (and you, dear reader, may partake of the glory *if* you desire and pursue the fullness of Christ) are going to be filled with the fullness of God in Christ through the Spirit. Just as Jesus eternally is filled with the presence, the love and the glory of God, so will we—when we have been prepared—be filled with the presence, the love and the glory of God in Christ.

> **22 "And the glory which thou gavest me I have given them; that they may be one, even as we are one:**
> **23 "I in them, and thou in me, that they may be made perfect in one; and that the world may know that thou hast sent me, and hast loved them, as thou hast loved me. . . ."**
>
> **—John 17**

TABERNACLES, AND THE WATER OF LIFE

We have seen that the Feast of Tabernacles parallels the new heaven and earth rule of Christ in that both are associated with the maturing of that which has been planted in the land of promise, to speak in a figure. Also, Tabernacles and the new heaven and earth rule bring to our mind the thought of God "tabernacling" in and with us.

A third area of salvation which is common to both the Feast of Tabernacles and the new heaven and earth Kingdom of Christ is that of the water of life (Revelation 22:1). The concept of the water of life is important in the Feast of Tabernacles, and also in the new earth.

The Feast of Tabernacles is closely associated with water. First of all, the feast was celebrated on the fifteenth through the twenty-second day of the seventh month, which occurred approximately during the last part of the month of September of our present calendar.

In terms of the climate of the Holy Land, the long dry season from May through August, relieved only by heavy summer dews, is about ended by the time of the Feast of Tabernacles. The early (former) rains are now at hand. The coming of rain brings about the replenishing of rivers, and speaks to us of the refreshing of the Holy Spirit as He comes to us and creates in us "rivers of living water."

Because the land of Israel is located in an area of the world where the availability of water is often a major concern, many of the passages of Scripture equate the blessing of God with an abundance of water.

> **11 And the LORD shall guide thee continually, and satisfy thy soul in drought, and make fat thy bones: and thou shalt be like a watered garden, and like a spring of water, whose waters fail not.**
>
> **—Isaiah 58**

> **18 And it shall come to pass in that day, *that* the mountains shall drop down new wine, and the hills shall flow with milk, and all the rivers of Judah shall flow with waters, and a fountain shall come forth of the house of the LORD, and shall water the valley of Shittim.**
>
> **—Joel 3**

> **13 Jesus answered and said unto her, "Whosoever drinketh of this water shall thirst again:**
> **14 "But whosoever drinketh of the water that I shall give him shall never thirst; but the water that I shall give him shall be in him a well of water springing up into everlasting life."**
> **—John 4**

The following words of Jesus have a direct bearing upon the celebration of Tabernacles:

> **37 In the last day, that great *day* of the feast, Jesus stood and cried, saying, "If any man thirst, let him come unto me, and drink.**
> **38 "He that believeth on me, as the scripture hath said, out of his belly shall flow rivers of living water."**
> **39 (But this spake he of the Spirit, which they that believe on him should receive: for the Holy Ghost was not yet *given;* because that Jesus was not yet glorified.)**
> **—John 7**

The "last day, that great day of the feast," was the eighth day of the Feast of Tabernacles (see note on John 7:37 by Reverend David Brown, *A Commentary on the Old and New Testaments;* Jamieson, Fausset, and Brown, Grand Rapids, Michigan: Wm. B. Eerdmans Publishing Co., 1945, Volume V, pp. 396, 397).

> **39 Also in the fifteenth day of the seventh month, when ye have gathered in the fruit of the land, ye shall keep a feast unto the LORD seven days: on the first day *shall be* a sabbath, and on the eighth day *shall be* a sabbath.**
> **—Leviticus 23**

"On the eighth day shall be a sabbath." The eighth day of Tabernacles is the "last day, that great day of the feast," of John 7:37. The eighth day of the Feast of Tabernacles is symbolic of the "first day" of eternity. After we have arrived at the perfect rest of God, as typified by the first seven days of Tabernacles, we have fulfilled a complete cycle, a "week" in which the total work of redemption has been accomplished in us.

On the "sixth day," so to speak, the Day of Atonement, we have been reconciled to God and created in the image of God. On the "seventh day" we have found rest in God and God has found rest in us—the direct result of our reconciliation to

God and our being created in His image. The sin which causes unrest has been rendered powerless and removed from our personality by the Holy Spirit.

But now we have come to the eighth day, the first day of the week which has no end. The new week is eternity and the eighth day of the Feast of Tabernacles signifies the beginning of our eternal priestly service to God Almighty, and our eternal reign as kings and priests over the nations of the earth.

In the days of Jesus the eighth day of Tabernacles was the "great day of the feast." It was the last day of the annual observance of the Levitical feasts and was celebrated with the greatest possible rejoicing.

One of the high points of the eight-day celebration of Tabernacles occurred each day as a priest brought water in golden vessels from the Pool of Siloam and the high priest poured the water into a basin on the Altar of Burnt Offering. On the eighth day trumpets were blown during the ceremony, and Isaiah 12:3 was sung: "with joy shall ye draw water out of the wells of salvation."

The Israelites were beside themselves with jubilation on this occasion. During the celebration Jesus stood in the midst and cried, "If any man thirst, let him come unto me, and drink. He that believeth on me, as the scripture hath said, out of his belly shall flow rivers of living water."

Although the Jews were taken up with their joy and thankfulness over the abundance of the harvest, were praying for and expecting the soon coming of the fall rains which would soften the sun-baked clods so that seed could be sown, and were ecstatic in general over the whole idea of the glory of God and their special relationship to Him, Jesus of Nazareth was exulting because of a circumstance unrealized as yet. In prophetic vision He saw the throne of the Almighty eternally established in Himself and His Wife, and the Holy Spirit of God issuing forth in a fathomless, uncrossable river, bringing life and healing to all who will drink.

Coming out from the throne of God and of the Lamb, which is to say out from the hearts of the saints, is the river of life which nourishes the peoples of the earth.

9 And it shall come to pass, *that* everything that liveth, which moveth, whithersoever the rivers shall come, shall live: and there shall be a very great multitude of fish, because these waters shall come thither: for they shall be healed; and every thing shall live whither the river cometh.

—Ezekiel 47

The "fish" are the multitudes of people converted through the glory of God coming upon the Church (John 17:21).

The spiritual fulfillment of the Levitical Feast of Tabernacles is portrayed in the twelfth chapter of Isaiah. The Lord Himself becomes our strength, our song and our salvation. It no longer is true that we are striving to gain these blessings from Him. As Tabernacles is fulfilled in us the Lord Jesus Christ enters into us and becomes these virtues.

THE LORD GOD OF HEAVEN IN JESUS CHRIST BECOMES OUR SALVATION!

1 AND in that day thou shalt say, O LORD, I will praise thee: though thou wast angry with me, thine anger is turned away, and thou confortedst me.

2 Behold, God *is* my salvation; I will trust, and not be afraid: for the LORD JEHOVAH *is* my strength and *my* song; he also is become my salvation.

3 Therefore with joy shall ye draw water out of the wells of salvation.

4 And in that day shall ye say, Praise the LORD, call upon his name, declare his doings among the people, make mention that his name is exalted.

5 Sing unto the LORD; for he hath done excellent things: this *is* known in all the earth.

6 Cry out and shout, thou inhabitant of Zion: for great *is* the Holy One of Israel in the midst of thee.

—Isaiah 12

When Jesus proclaimed, "He that believeth on me, as the scripture hath said, out of his belly shall flow rivers of living water," He could have been referring to Isaiah 58:11, or Joel 3:18, or Ezekiel 47:1. But it seems to us that Jesus had in mind the twelfth chapter of Isaiah. The "wells of salvation" are the members of the Body of Christ, and the saints bring forth the waters of eternal life with great joy. Truly, the "Holy One of Israel" is great "in the midst of" each inhabitant of Zion.

The Feast of Pentecost typifies the outpouring of the Holy Spirit upon us and the Feast of Tabernacles typifies the springing up of the well within us. It is interesting to note that the waters of judgment in the days of Noah came up from the earth as well as down from the heavens: "the same day were all the fountains of the great deep broken up, and the windows of heaven were opened" (Genesis 7:11). In the Day of the Lord the water of life will flow forth from the Christians as well as down from heaven.

The tree of our life is planted with the help of the refreshing rains of Pentecost. But the saving, healing fruit of our tree becomes available to the peoples of the earth at Tabernacles. Pentecost is associated with the Holy Place of the Tabernacle of the Congregation, thus with the gifts and ministries of the Church. Tabernacles is associated with the Holy of Holies, thus with the Ark of the Covenant and the full, clear communication of the glory of God.

The Millennium is a Pentecost of Pentecosts, and the Church will be brought to maturity during that period. The new heaven and earth rule of Christ is a Tabernacle of Tabernacles; and the fullness of the Father, the fullness of the Son, the fullness of the Holy Spirit, and the total, complete perfection of the Wife of the Lamb—all will shine forth in unabridged splendor, revelation and communication throughout eternity.

ETERNAL SERVICE TO GOD

The concept of eternal service to God as His royal priest is a fourth aspect of the Christian salvation which is common to both the Levitical Feast of Tabernacles and the new heaven and earth reign of Jesus Christ. The whole nation of Israel was a "kingdom of priests" before God.

> **5 Now therefore, if ye will obey my voice indeed, and keep my covenant, then ye shall be a peculiar treasure unto me above all people: for all the earth *is* mine:**

6 And ye shall be unto me a kingdom of priests, and an holy nation. These *are* the words which thou shalt speak unto the children of Israel.

—Exodus 19

By commanding the Israelites to leave their houses for seven days each year and live outside in booths made with tree branches, God was leading them to face the reality that they were not like the other nations of the earth. The Jewish family indeed had some astonishing historical events to call to mind—events which to this day are deeply meaningful, not only to the person who is Jewish by birth, but also to the Christian saints.

A man named Abraham, living in one of the large cities of his time, was singled out by the Lord and commanded to leave his home and go forth into a strange country. God appeared to him on several occasions and required holy living of him—holy in the sense of personal devotion to a personal God.

God blessed Abraham and his family, and after two generations his descendants went down to live in Egypt because of famine in the land to which Abraham had been called. Several hundred years later, when the descendants of Abraham were numbered in the hundreds of thousands, the same Lord revealed Himself to Moses and called Abraham's children to leave Egypt and go forth into a strange country just as He, the Lord, had required of Abraham in the first place. Egypt, refusing to let God's servants go, was destroyed in the process.

Never before nor since has God revealed Himself and blessed an entire nation of people after this fashion. Never before had God sacrificed one people in order that a second people might come to worship, serve and know Him. Never before had God formed a highway in the midst of the sea, caused water to flow forth from a rock, fed a hungry multitude with bread from the heavens. No other country of people had received commandments and ordinances which regulated the conduct of daily living.

Never before had God led one nation of people into the homeland of another nation, helping the invaders to destroy the inhabitants who were defending their families, houses and lands. Israel, and Israel alone, has a history that a person can meditate upon for seventy years, let alone the seven days of Tabernacles, and never reach the depth of its significance.

Each one of the seven Levitical feasts is designed to bring home the truth that Israel is a called-out people, a nation of priests. All the peoples of the earth belong to the Lord. But Israel belongs to God in a special way, and the Church is part of that same Seed of Abraham.

The Feast of Tabernacles, with its requirement for living in booths, portrays in a dramatic manner that the nation of Israel plays a unique role among the peoples of the earth. Israel is a "kingdom of priests, and a holy nation," a "peculiar treasure" unto God above all other persons.

The priestly responsibilities and privileges of Abraham in his day, of Abraham's descendants at a later period, of the Christians now and during the Millennium, will be brought to magnificent fulfillment in the new heaven and earth. The Wife of the Lamb, the new Jerusalem, will be immersed in the fullness of God Almighty, will gaze in resurrection purity upon God's face, and will serve and represent Him throughout the ages of ages, world without end.

Christ Himself is going to write upon each overcomer the name of God, the name of the new Jerusalem, and Christ's new name (Revelation 3:12). The purpose of these three names is to seal forever and ever the identity of the individual. He now belongs to and is an indivisible part of God.

The overcomer is a pillar in the Temple of God, a supporting, integral, essential element of the structure. Apart from him the building collapses; it is marred, losing its symmetry and perfection. Each overcomer is an inseparable unit of God's dwelling place in the earth.

Christ writes upon each overcomer the new name of Christ. What that new name of Christ is we do not know. But he who bears the name of Christ is of the living Being and Presence of God Almighty. Christ is All and in all in the new heaven and earth, and they who have His new name written upon themselves are His Presence wherever they may go (Galatians 2:20).

The peoples of the new heaven and earth will recognize the priests of God. They will understand that God has sent Christ and has loved those whom Christ has chosen as He has loved Christ (John 17:23).

> **3 And the Gentiles shall come to thy light, and kings to the brightness of thy rising.**
>
> **—Isaiah 60**

> **6 But ye shall be named the Priests of the LORD: *men* shall call you the Ministers of our God: ye shall eat the riches of the Gentiles, and in their glory shall ye boast yourselves.**
>
> **—Isaiah 61**

> **9 And their seed shall be known among the Gentiles, and their offspring among the people: all that see them shall acknowledge them, that they *are* the seed *which* the LORD hath blessed.**
>
> **—Isaiah 61**

The new Jerusalem, the holy city, the Wife of the Lamb, will be a "kingdom of priests, and a holy nation" among the nations of the earth.

> **3 And there shall be no more curse: but the throne of God and of the Lamb shall be in it; and his servants shall serve him:**
>
> **4 And they shall see his face; and his name *shall be* in their foreheads.**
>
> **—Revelation 22**

The members of the Body of Christ will serve God throughout eternity. This is the fulfillment of the eighth day of the Feast of Tabernacles, the eighth day representing the first day of the new week of eternity. It is a new week because the entire memory of the fall of Adam and Eve, and the subsequent thousands of years of rebellion and uncleanness, tragedy and anguish, will have been erased from the consciousness of the peoples of the earth.

From the original rebellion in heaven to the fiery judgment upon Gog and Magog, the total guilt, tendency and history of sin will have been purged from the earth. All evildoers will have found their place in the lake of fire. The family of God will be so united in the fullness of His glory that resistance to His will shall be unthinkable. Every creature and every thing in creation will be radiant with the beauty of Christ.

The concept of a priest is that of a person who represents

God to people, and people to God. We have to have considerable experience as a believer before we can bring God's grace and glory to another person. When we attempt to minister to another person in the times of deepest need we are as a "tinkling cymbal" if we have never had fiery trials ourselves. When Paul exhorts us in Philippians to "Rejoice in the Lord alway," and we understand that he was a prisoner in Rome and being closely guarded at the time, then we can take heart in the hour of tribulation. Isn't it so?

But our real problem as a priest arises when we approach God in order to render priestly service directly to Him. Our God is so holy that the efforts of humans to please Him, no matter how sincere and conscientious those efforts may be, can never be perfectly acceptable. We humans are so utterly inadequate that we can only cast ourselves upon His mercy. Thousands of years of travail have been necessary in order to bring forth God's kings and priests, the Body of Messiah, the Temple of God, the Wife of the Lamb.

We would have no hope at all of becoming an eternal servant of the Lord if it were not for the precious redeeming blood of Jesus Christ. Through Him—and only through Him—we have boldness to enter into the very presence of God and to present our needs before the throne. Our access to the throne in prayer, through the blood of Christ, marks the beginning of our acquaintance with the Father (Hebrews 4:16).

Calvary provided us with the price of our redemption, and with the living Substance of God which we must eat continually if we are to be created a servant of the Lord. The Substance of Christ is the Divine gold which must be refined! refined! refined! in us through endless testing, night and day, day after day, year after year. The ministries and gifts of the Church groan in travail as the burden of the Lord comes to us, transforming us, guiding us, rebuking us. All of the fiery furnaces of affliction and the desolate wildernesses to which we are subjected are the crucible in which the gold of God must be refined.

In the meanwhile the Seed of Christ is growing in our hearts, and the Holy Spirit is invading and taking over the life processes in us. We are being created in the image of Christ.

There is not one element of our being which is not of the greatest interest to God and which will not be subjected to the most intense scrutiny of the Godhead. For we are being made the eternal priests of God Almighty and must be able to dwell in the consuming fire forever and ever.

As soon as we have been received into the Millennial Kingdom we will have a thousand years of exposure to the glory of God—that blazing Holiness which transfigured the face of Moses, at which no man can gaze and live. Yet, we will be bathed in that holy Fire for one thousand years.

The prolonged exposure to God's glory will season and mature the Divine gold in us. The glass-like transparency, so prominent in the new Jerusalem, will characterize our personality. Still, we will scarecely be able to minister before Him as Christ ministers before Him. We are speaking now of the Ancient of Days, the Father of our Lord Jesus Christ, at the memory of Whom the demons tremble in utter terror.

One day we will be able to see Him in the Face. One day we will be prepared to minister to Him and to have His name impressed in our personality—body, soul and spirit. He dwells forever in the beauty of His holiness—that same holiness which now is being created within us.

The holiness of God includes more than refraining from indulging in a prescribed list of specific behaviors. The radiant beauty of holiness is the transparent Nature of God Himself. There is no darkness, no uncleanness whatever, in the Nature of God. His holiness is so pure, so clean, so shining, so blameless, so loving, so single-minded in purpose and intention, that we by contrast are seen to be very small and mean.

Indeed, we have been called by God to be a holy nation, a royal priesthood. Seeing then that God has called us unto Himself, to love Him alone, to be a peculiar treasure unto Him out of all the peoples of the earth, should we not lay aside all other ambitions and enthusiasms and direct the springs of our desires and energies toward waiting diligently upon His every desire? It will require our whole attention and willingness if we are to bear faithfully with the rigorous training to which we are being subjected.

But we must, as did Paul, have respect unto the glory which is to be ours provided we endure in patient faithfulness the circumstances which God sends our way. To minister as a priest before the living God is a calling so high that no other destiny can be compared with it in any manner whatever. Whoever has difficulty deciding which calling to pursue, that of God or that of his own, will have a great deal of trouble until he makes up his mind. God will not be put off indefinitely, and He is jealous over them whom He has chosen.

Let us Christians, each having been chosen as a priest of God Almighty, see to it that we make waiting upon the Lord the first business of our life. If we do, His educational program will result in our being able to behold His very Face forever and to represent Him throughout His creation unto the ages of ages, world without end.

We have mentioned that the Feast of Tabernacles parallels the new heaven and earth rule of Christ in that each is associated with the maturing of all crops sown in the land of promise. We have discussed the fact that both the Feast of Tabernacles and the new heaven and earth rule of Christ have to do with the "tabernacling" of God with mankind. The thought has been presented that the water of life, with the tree of life growing along its banks, is also a part of the Feast of Tabernacles and of the new heaven and earth.

The role of priestly service to God was emphasized in the annual dwelling in booths of the Israelite families. The perfection of priestly service will occur when "his servants shall serve him" in the new Jerusalem.

TABERNACLES, AND THE LAW OF GOD

There is another area of salvation which is common to the Levitical Feast of Tabernacles and the new heaven and earth reign of Jesus Christ. The area is that of the law of God. The Feast of Tabernacles is associated with the formal, oral reading of the law to every Israelite, from the youngest to the oldest, and to the non-Israelite who was sojourning among them at the time.

> **9 And Moses wrote this law, and delivered it unto the priests the sons of Levi, which bare the ark of the covenant of the LORD, and unto all the elders of Israel.**
>
> **10 And Moses commanded them, saying, At the end of *every* seven years, in the solemnity of the year of release, in the feast of tabernacles,**
>
> **11 When all Israel is come to appear before the LORD thy God in the place which he shall choose, thou shalt read this law before all Israel in their hearing.**
>
> **12 Gather the people together, men, and women, and children, and thy stranger that *is* within thy gates, that they may hear, and that they may learn, and fear the LORD your God, and observe all the words of this law:**
>
> **13 And *that* their children, which have not known *any thing*, may hear, and learn to fear the LORD your God, as long as ye live in the land whither ye go over Jordan to possess it.**
>
> **—Deuteronomy 31**

Notice in the above passage that Israel was to assemble "in the place which he shall choose," that is to say, in the place which God shall choose. The place which God has chosen for the revealing of the perfect expression of His law is the new earth. The holiness of the holy city, the new Jerusalem, is the perfect expression and fruition of God's law. The beauty of the holy city is the beauty of holiness.

> **9 O worship the LORD in the beauty of holiness: fear before him all the earth.**
>
> **—Psalms 96**

Every man, woman, boy and girl of Israel was to hear the law, to learn the law, to fear the Lord, and to obey the law. Also, the "stranger that is within thy gates," typical of the nations of the earth, must come to understand and act in accordance with the utter holiness of the Lord God of Israel.

Thus the law of God was brought before the people "at the end of every seven years, in the solemnity of the year of release, in the feast of tabernacles."

The law was given in the wilderness by the hand of Moses, but the law was pointed expressly at moral behavior in the land of promise, which was to be under the supervision of Joshua and the judges who followed Joshua, and then under the kings of Israel.

Notice in particular the directive: "as long as ye live in the land whither ye go over Jordan to possess it." The lessons in holiness which the Holy Spirit is teaching us are given in order to guide our conduct now, and will continue to guide our conduct throughout the coming Kingdom age and on into the new heaven and earth rule of Christ.

Every bit of personal righteousness, holiness and obedience of behavior which is being developed in us at this time will have direct application in the age to come, and has far-reaching consequences as far as our position in the Kingdom of Christ is concerned.

> **19 "Whosoever therefore shall break one of these least commandments, and shall teach men so, he shall be called the least in the kingdom of heaven: but whosoever shall do and teach *them*, the same shall be called great in the kingdom of heaven. . . ."**
>
> **—Matthew 5**

> **14 Ye have said, It *is* vain to serve God: and what profit *is it* that we have kept his ordinance, and that we have walked mournfully before the LORD of hosts?**
>
> **15 And now we call the proud happy; yea, they that work wickedness are set up; yea, *they that* tempt God are even delivered.**
>
> **16 Then they that feared the LORD spake often one to another: and the LORD hearkened, and heard *it*, and a book of remembrance was written before him for them that feared the LORD, and that thought upon his name.**
>
> **17 And they shall be mine, saith the LORD of hosts, in that day when I make up my jewels; and I will spare them, as a man spareth his own son that serveth him.**
>
> **18 Then shall ye return, and discern between the righteous and the wicked, between him that serveth God and him that serveth him not.**
>
> **—Malachi 3**

> **3 And they that be wise shall shine as the brightness of the firmament; and they that turn many to righteousness as the stars for ever and ever.**
>
> **—Daniel 12**

> **8 For bodily exercise profiteth little: but godliness is profitable unto all things, having promise of the life that now is, and of that which is to come.**
>
> **—I Timothy 4**

We are being made in the moral image of Christ now so that we can rule in righteousness (the rod of iron) throughout the Millennial Jubilee, and so that we can radiate the beauty of holiness in the new heaven and earth rule of Christ.

The eighth chapter of Nehemiah is a prophetic picture of the coming of the law of God into the earth. Notice that the ministers and the people were all in their places on this occasion:

> **73 So the priests, and the Levites, and the porters, and the singers, and *some* of the people, and the Nethinims, and all Israel, dwelt in their cities; and when the seventh month** [the month of Trumpets, Day of Atonement and Tabernacles] **came, the children of Israel *were* in their cities.**
>
> **—Nehemiah 7**

It is true of us Christians today that as soon as we have made some headway against sin and the enemy (as typified by the rebuilding of the wall of Jerusalem—Nehemiah 7:1), then we should be looking to the Lord for opportunities to bring the knowledge of God and of His holy ways to other people (as typified by the eighth chapter of Nehemiah).

There is not a clearer picture of the Day of the Lord found in the Bible than the portrayal set forth in Nehemiah 8. Notice the first verse:

> **1 AND all the people gathered themselves together as one man into the street that *was* before the water gate; and they spake unto Ezra the scribe to bring the book of the law of Moses, which the LORD had commanded to Israel.**

It was now possible for "all the people" to gather themselves together "as one man" into the street that was before the "water gate." The wall (against sin, to speak symbolically) had been built. The Lord's servants were set in their places for the work of the ministry. The "peoples of the earth" were gathered together to drink of the water of life.

The people came to hear Ezra read the law of Moses. What a scene this is! Ezra represents the Church. The people represent the nations of the earth who will come to the Church to learn of God.

> **16 And it shall come to pass, *that* every one that is left of all the nations which came against Jerusalem shall even go up from year to year to worship the King, the LORD of hosts, and to keep the feast of tabernacles.**
>
> **—Zechariah 14**

Ezra's reading of the law took place on the first day of the seventh month, the convocation of Trumpets, and continued through the week of the Feast of Tabernacles (Nehemiah 8:18). So we see that the last three of the Levitical convocations—Trumpets, Day of Atonement and Tabernacles—are associated in significance with the establishing of God's law, God's Kingdom, in the earth.

The most complete expression of the relationship between the Levitical feasts and the law of God will occur in the kingdom-wide fulfillment of the Feast of Tabernacles, which is the new heaven and earth rule of Jesus Christ. The purpose of the law of God is to produce holiness of behavior. The most complete expression of God's holiness which heaven and earth will ever see is the holy city, the Wife of the Lamb, the new Jerusalem. The holiness of the new Jerusalem is the holiness of Jesus Christ Himself.

Notice that the "water gate" and the law of Moses are linked together in Nehemiah 8:1. That is because the Holy Spirit, Who is the water of life, is the heavenly Power Who enables us to live righteously and thus fulfill the intent of the law. The Holy Spirit judges us, delivers us, heals us, and enables us to live in righteousness, holiness and obedience to the Father.

THE LIGHT OF THE WORLD

Light was an important feature of the celebration of the Feast of Tabernacles. The new Jerusalem will be filled with the light of the glory of God in Christ.

At the time of Jesus it was a custom during the Feast of Tabernacles for the Jews to come to the Temple carrying torches. Candlesticks were lighted in the Temple of Herod. The result of the combining of the torches of the worshippers with the candlesticks of the Temple was a flood of light which lit up the surrounding area, just as will be true when the light of the glory of God, at the coming of our Lord Jesus Christ, is combined with the inner lights of each of the Christian believers.

It was in the context of the torches and candlesticks of the celebration of Tabernacles that the Jews could understand the meaning of Jesus when He presented His Church as the light of the world.

> **14 "Ye are the light of the world. A city that is set on an hill cannot be hid. . . ."**
>
> **—Matthew 5**

> **16 "Let your light so shine before men, that they may see your good works, and glorify your Father which is in heaven. . . ."**
>
> **—Matthew 5**

There are at least three dimensions of the light which is to shine forth from the Body of Christ: (1) Christ shining forth through the Church in godly behavior; (2) Christ shining forth through the Church in supernatural power and revelation; and (3) Christ shining forth through the Church in teaching concerning the Person, purpose and way of God. These three constitute what the Church is in moral character; what the Church can do; and what the Church states.

The "good works" which mankind sees in the saint of God are those actions which spring from the nature which has been transformed by the Holy Spirit and filled with the Substance of Christ: good deeds performed in love; the maintaining of a joyful spirit in all kinds of difficulties; peace in the midst of turmoil; patience in the face of threats and belligerence; self-control and temperance in the use of the world; cleanliness of speech and behavior (Galatians 5:22, 23). These good works enable the people of the world to gain understanding of the true character of God. They are the light in the darkness of this present hour.

The supernatural works of power which the Christian

Church is enabled to perform, serve as a light to the world. Divine wisdom and knowledge—faith which comes from God and which brings about God's intervention in circumstances; extraordinary healings and miracles which temporarily set aside the laws of nature; oracular utterance which reveals the mind of God; the ability to discern the good and evil spirits which are active in a given situation; instantly-gained ability to speak and understand foreign languages—these are the Lampstand of the Tabernacle of the Congregation, to speak figuratively. Supernatural manifestations of wisdom and power are the shining forth of the glory of the Spirit of God in the material world (I Corinthians 12:8-10).

The light of Christ shone not only through the moral perfection of His Nature but also through the miraculous signs with which His ministry was surrounded. If Christ had been morally perfect but had not performed miraculous deeds He would have been the world's greatest teacher and example of how people should conduct themselves, but He would not have been the Teacher from God.

On the other hand, if Christ had worked His many miracles but was not morally perfect, it would have been evident that He came from another world but there would have been a question as to which world He came from. Also He would not, of course, have been able to serve as our spotless Lamb of God Who takes away the sin of the world.

What the Church is and does in moral character and behavior is one dimension of the light of the world. What the Church is able to perform in the area of miraculous works of power is a second dimension of the light of the world.

A church made up of members who are morally perfect but who are not exercising works of Divine power may be the world's greatest example of righteous living, but part of the Divine witness is lacking. A church composed of members who perform supernatural works in Jesus' name but who are careless about their moral conduct is in contact with spiritual power, but the testimony is sullied and the members will be lost if they do not repent. God cannot work out His plan of redemption when His people are continuing in uncleanness and unrighteousness.

The third aspect of the light which is to shine forth from the Body of Christ concerns what the Church has to say about God's attitude and plan with regard to the peoples of the earth. The Church possesses the truth of God.

> **15 That ye may be blameless and harmless, the sons of God without rebuke, in the midst of a crooked and perverse nation, among whom ye shine as lights in the world;**
> **16 Holding forth the word of life; that I may rejoice in the day of Christ, that I have not run in vain, neither laboured in vain.**
> **—Philippians 2**

As the spiritual darkness is settling upon the earth in our day, just before the coming of our Lord Jesus Christ, there appears to be a growing willingness of people to openly mock and scorn the Lord Jesus Christ and His teachings.

God, of course, knew well in advance that all of this darkness would come about. He always is in perfect control of every situation because of His unlimited power and foreknowledge. God never gives up on what He sets out to do. God never changes.

It is the will of God that the peoples of the earth walk in accordance with the laws of His Kingdom. The laws of His Kingdom are the guides to human conduct which Jesus presented in the Sermon on the Mount. How then, in view of the fact that people are moving further away from rather than closer to these guides, is God going to have His way in the earth?

God is moving according to the principle of the firstfruits. First came Jesus. He is the One Who perfectly observed the laws of the Kingdom of God in the earth. Think of it! One man among the hundreds of millions of the earth. Yet He walked without fault, keeping all the laws of the Kingdom of God.

Next, the saints of the Lord are being guided and strengthened by the Holy Spirit so that they can begin to keep the laws of the Kingdom. It is not easy, and it means a complete overthrowing of the works of darkness in our lives. How our flesh kicks and rebels! But little by little, line upon line, precept upon precept, teaching upon teaching, the Spirit of God is converting us from the inside out.

The Holy Spirit commences in the core of our being, in our "holy of holies," creating Christ in us. Our total conversion from our wild fleshly nature to a person who walks in the Spirit of God does not happen overnight. But if we follow the Spirit of God as He brings us to Christ, then our total conversion to righteous, holy and obedient conduct is as certain as the promises of God in Christ.

First, Christ. Then, every member of the Church, including the smallest and weakest of the believers (Isaiah 60:21, 22; Song of Solomon 7:8, 9; Luke 7:28; Hebrews 8:11)—every one will be created a priest of God Almighty, a person who lives, moves and has his being in the righteous and holy ways of the Lord.

But what about the nations of the earth? Are they forever doomed to live in lust, idolatry, covetousness, murder, strife, filthiness of speech and mind, bitterness of spirit, as we see today? Not so! The righteousness which God is creating in the Church, His Temple, the righteousness which proceeds from Christ in us, will be ministered to the nations of the earth through God's kings and priests—His Church. The nations will learn of God from the Church. This is one of the great purposes which God has for the existence of the Church.

> **3 And many people shall go and say, Come ye, and let us go up to the mountain of the LORD, to the house of the God of Jacob; and he will teach us of his ways, and we will walk in his paths: for out of Zion shall go forth the law, and the word of the LORD from Jerusalem.**
>
> **—Isaiah 2**

> **5 Then thou shalt see, and flow together, and thine heart shall fear, and be enlarged; because the abundance of the sea shall be converted unto thee, the forces of the Gentiles shall come unto thee.**
>
> **—Isaiah 60**

Christ is Truth. In Him are hidden all the treasures of wisdom and knowledge. Those who come to Him find the understanding needed to solve every problem, the key to every mystery, the way out of every dilemma. Christ is the Light of God shining in the darkness of this world. We have Him in our hearts and so there is light in us.

All who would have light must come to Christ in the Church for there is no other light which can illumine the darkness in mankind. His light is His law, and to "see" His way is to be conformed to His holiness. Such is the fulfillment of the law of God. In His light we see light.

God's glory is light. The new Jerusalem is filled with the fullness of the glory of God, therefore with the fullness of His light. So complete is the light of God that there is no more need of the sun or moon to give light upon the earth.

> **23 And the city had no need of the sun, neither of the moon, to shine in it: for the glory of God did lighten it, and the Lamb *is* the light thereof.**
>
> **24 And the nations of them which are saved shall walk in the light of it: and the kings of the earth do bring their glory and honour into it.**
>
> **—Revelation 21**

In the beginning, Christ was the light of the world. There were the evenings and the mornings until the fourth day. On the fourth day the sun, moon and stars were created. How could there have been evenings and mornings apart from the existence of the sun? The answer is that Christ gave light to the earth until the heavenly bodies were created.

In the new heaven and earth rule of Christ He again will be the light of the world. His saints will have Him dwelling in themselves; therefore His light will shine from them and illumine the entire world.

> **1 FOR Zion's sake will I not hold my peace, and for Jerusalem's sake I will not rest, until the righteousness thereof go forth as brightness, and the salvation thereof as a lamp *that* burneth.**
>
> **—Isaiah 62**

15

The Last Feast and the Christian

The last three of the seven convocations of the Lord are *Trumpets* (Leviticus 23:24); the *Day of Atonement* (Leviticus 23:27); and *Tabernacles* (Leviticus 23:34). The three experiences typified by these three convocations interact in us until we become the Temple of the Lord.

Trumpets, coming just after Pentecost, speaks of our spiritual resurrection from the dead, and also of spiritual warfare. As the Christian believer learns to enter into the Holy Spirit he is raised from the dead in the spiritual sense, and will be raised in the physical sense at the return of Jesus Christ.

Our being raised from the dead spiritually brings us into judgment. The more we are raised the more clearly we can see our own sins of the flesh and our disobediences to God's will. When we see our sins and disobediences we are to confess them, turn away from them, resist the devil, and submit to God. This is our personal experience of the *Day of Atonement.*

Confession and repentance cleanses our personalities, thus making room in our hearts for a further growth of Christ within us, Christ within us being the fulfillment of the Feast of *Tabernacles.*

As we receive more of Christ within us we are raised yet further from the dead, spiritually speaking. We keep on coming to know the "power of his resurrection." This increased resurrection life causes us to become conscious of the sins and disobediences remaining in our lives. We then proceed to confess, repent and turn to God with increased diligence and thoroughness. This further repentance and submission make way for an even greater growth of Christ—the Resurrection—within us.

It is the will of the Lord that this process continue until Christ has been fully developed within us, making us eligible to be filled with all the fullness of God.

It is the author's understanding that the Pentecostal experience, along with the basic salvation experience, is being promulgated widely throughout the earth today. And, of course, we must never let up on the task of bringing the Gospel of Christ to every man, woman, boy and girl upon the face of the earth.

In addition, it appears that the Holy Spirit is ready now to bring believers who have come as far as Pentecost on to the fulfillments of the remaining three convocations of the Lord, in the manner which we have just described. The Holy Spirit will not cease working with the Church until the Church is without spot or wrinkle.

It is our point of view that Jesus through the Spirit will continue to perfect the Church until His coming in the clouds of glory, and that this process of perfecting will take place throughout the darkest hours of earth's history—those days of the fullness of sin which even now are coming upon us.

The Lord Jesus is coming in His *external* kingdom and every eye shall see Him. But the issue of the present hour, as far as the Church is concerned, is the perfecting of the *internal* kingdom. As soon as we are under His precious blood the Lord is able to have fellowship *with* us. But the Feast of Tabernacles points toward the Lord's presence *in* us.

The Lord's presence *in* us is the all-important work of the Holy Spirit as He brings us through the processes of salvation. Christ is going to appear *in* His Church, as well as visibly to the world, in order that the Church may bring the presence and glory of God to the peoples of the earth.

The internal kingdom must be perfected in us *before* the external kingdom appears from heaven. That is how we know that Christ is not going to appear just yet. It is because His internal kingdom has not been perfected in the Church.

If Christ desired only an external kingdom He would have returned long ago. But Christ is seeking to take up residence in the Body of Christ, and for that reason the Body must be perfected. The Body of Christ has not as yet been perfected. There is more of God for us.

As the dark clouds gather over the earth there is coming an entrance of Christ into His temple—the Christian Church. It does not matter that Satan will become incarnate in a man who will sit in the holy of holies of an earthly temple. God in Christ is coming to the Body of Christ and His vessels will have an inner glory vastly exceeding anything that Antichrist can produce.

This inner manifestation of the Lord's presence will take place, as we understand it, before the resurrection of the dead at Christ's coming, and is a necessary forerunner of and preparation for the first resurrection—the resurrection of the saints.

Let us look now at the Scriptures, both Old and New Testaments, to see what the Holy Spirit has said about the internal dimension of the Kingdom of God.

> **19 "Yet a little while, and the world seeth me no nore; but ye see me: because I live, ye shall live also.**
> **20 "At that day ye shall know that I *am* in my Father, and ye in me, and I in you. . . ."**
>
> **—John 14**

We can notice from the above passage that this particular manifestation of the Lord can be witnessed only by the disciples and not at all by the world. His life becomes our life.

> **21 "He that hath my commandments, and keepeth them, he it is that loveth me: and he that loveth me shall be loved of my Father, and I will love him, and will manifest myself to him."**
>
> **—John 14**

The inner manifestation of Christ cannot be obtained by the average church-attender. It can be obtained only by the sincere disciple of Jesus Christ—the person who keeps Christ's commandments.

The question which would arise naturally after hearing such a promise was stated by Judas.

> **22 Judas saith unto him, not Iscariot, Lord, how is it that thou wilt manifest thyself unto us, and not unto the world?**
>
> **—John 14**

How can Christ show Himself to us without being seen by the world? How is this possible?

The answer is, Christ is going to come to each disciple in an inner revelation, in fulfillment of the Feast of Tabernacles. If we follow the pattern of the feasts of the Lord we come to the conclusion that this experience will come *after* Pentecost because the Feast of Tabernacles came after the Feast of Pentecost.

> **23 Jesus answered and said unto him, "If a man love me, he will keep my words: and my Father will love him, and we will come unto him, and make our abode with him. . . ."**
>
> **–John 14**

It is our understanding that the "Tabernacles" experience of the indwelling of the Father and the Son in the saints will take place before the resurrection of the dead, before the change in the mortal body, and that such indwelling will enable the saints –God's remnant–to be more than a match for anything that Satan is able to bring forth on the earth during the last days.

We see this concept cropping up throughout the writings of the prophets of Israel. Notice the second and third chapters of Joel, for example. In Joel 2:31 we have a pronouncement concerning the turning of the sun into darkness and the moon into blood–two events which we know will occur just before the return of Christ in the clouds of glory.

But look what else is going to be true during those darkest of days!

> **32 And it shall come to pass, *that* whosoever shall call on the name of the LORD shall be delivered: for in mount Zion and in Jerusalem shall be deliverance, as the LORD hath said, and in the remnant whom the LORD shall call.**
>
> **–Joel 2**

In other words, at the darkest hour of earth's history, just before the return of Christ, there will be power in Zion–the Body of Christ–to deliver "whosoever shall call on the name of the Lord."

Again, in Chapter 3 of Joel:

> **15 The sun and the moon shall be darkened, and the stars shall withdraw their shining.**
>
> **16 The LORD also shall roar out of Zion, and utter his voice from Jerusalem; and the heavens and the earth shall shake: but the LORD *will* be the hope of his people, and the strength of the children of Israel.**

At the moment of what appears to be the greatest defeat for the Kingdom of God the Lord will take His place in the Church and roar back defiantly against the enemy. Instead of weakness in that hour there will be the hope and strength of the Lord which will make each believer a Divine powerhouse of victory over the worst the enemy can perform.

It is our point of view that the preparation for this entrance of the fullness of Christ into His Church has begun already, as in the world sin is descending to foul depths. The impact of the Holy Spirit's work in us is that we are learning to confess our sins, opening up the doors of our hearts so that the Lord Jesus can enter into us to an increasingly greater degree.

> **1 BEHOLD, I will send my messenger, and he shall prepare the way before me: and the Lord, whom ye seek, shall suddenly come to his temple, even the messenger of the covenant, whom ye delight in: behold, he shall come, saith the LORD of hosts.**
>
> **2 But who may abide the day of his coming? and who shall stand when he appeareth? for he *is* like a refiner's fire, and like fullers' soap:**
>
> **—Malachi 3**

The temple of the Lord is the Body of Christ. As we begin to lift up the everlasting doors of our hearts the Lord of hosts enters in, ready to do battle against His enemies. Therefore, we have to confess our sins and repent so that Christ can settle down to rest within us.

Again, we notice the association of the glory of God with the darkest hour of earth's history:

> **1 FOR, behold the day cometh, that shall burn as an oven; and all the proud, yea, and all that do wickedly, shall be stubble: and the day that cometh shall burn them up, saith the LORD of hosts, that it shall leave them neither root nor branch.**
>
> **2 But unto you that fear my name shall the Sun of righteousness arise with healing in his wings; and ye shall go forth, and grow up as calves of the stall.**
>
> **—Malachi 4**

Notice that the destruction of the wicked upon the earth is associated with the healing of God's people and with their growth to maturity.

Isaiah informs us of the manner in which God in the Head and Body of Christ, Who is the Servant of the Lord, is going to respond to the maturing of wickedness in the earth.

> **13 The LORD shall go forth as a mighty man, he shall stir up jealousy like a man of war: he shall cry, yea, roar; he shall prevail against his enemies.**
>
> **—Isaiah 42**

When will God "go forth as a mighty man"? When will He "cry, yea, roar"? When will He "prevail against his enemies"? When will all this take place?

It will happen during the night in which no man can work. The preparation for the going forth of the Lord is occurring now as we allow the Lord Jesus to enter into our hearts to the fullest extent, giving ourselves over to Him in strict obedience and diligent discipleship.

If we thus accept Christ as Lord over us, the Father and the Son will make their abode with us. In the meanwhile the peoples of the earth will bring themselves down to the lowest cesspools of filth, even as we see in our day. This sin and rebellion will bring down upon the earth the judgments of God.

Then, at the appointed hour, the Father in the Son will "roar" out through the Church. The saints of the Lord will be the vessels which God will use to bring utter destruction upon the kingdom of darkness.

Isaiah teaches us that the darkest hour to come upon the earth will be the occasion for the greatest light to come upon the saints of Christ.

> **2 For, behold, the darkness shall cover the earth, and gross darkness the people: but the LORD shall arise upon thee, and his glory shall be seen upon thee.**
>
> **—Isaiah 60**

We Christians are to see to it that we do not allow ourselves to become troubled or afraid no matter what we see coming to pass upon the earth. Rather, we are to dwell "in the secret place of the Most High." If we will keep ourselves in the center of the will of Christ, serving Him with all diligence, then the protection of the Lord will cover us. The plagues of judgment will not come near us. No evil shall befall us.

We can hide ourselves under the wings of the Almighty God.

> **20 Come, my people, enter thou into thy chambers, and shut thy doors about thee: hide thyself as it were for a little moment, until the indignation be overpast.**
>
> **—Isaiah 26**

By receiving the fullness of God's presence into our lives we will become pillars of strength, a great help to the weaker Christians and to the unsaved who will be tossed to and fro upon the waters of violence and lust which are rising in the earth. We will be prepared, as was Joseph, to nourish the family of God in the time of famine through means of the "manna" which Christ will pour into our souls.

No matter how dark the hour there will be light in the hearts of all the saints, just as Goshen remained lighted when Egypt was wrapped in thick darkness. Our light will be the Father and the Son Who will be dwelling gloriously within us and dining with us upon the unlimited abundance of the internal kingdom.

Then, at a moment which will catch the ungodly unprepared, God in Christ will rise up in the Church. The Lord will roar out of Zion. He will bring terrible destruction upon His enemies. The Lord Jesus will descend from heaven and the powers of darkness will find themselves encircled on every hand by both the internal and the external ferocity of the Kingdom of God.

Christ will be *in* the saints, saving those who call upon the name of the Lord. Christ will be *with* the saints, coming in external form upon the clouds so that every eye shall see Him. The external Christ, the avenging Lamb, will hurl down the thunderbolts of God upon the wicked. Their destruction will be total. The memory of sin will be wiped clean from the planet Earth.

Then will the creation break forth into singing. All of nature will be released into the glorious liberty of the children of God. The saints will have God and Christ eternally within them, and God and Christ without in the external kingdom. Can you think of anything more wonderful than that?

"So shall we ever be with the Lord"! Hallelujah!

ANOTHER OUTSTANDING BOOK ON THIS SAME SUBJECT

YOU CAN OVERCOME

This outstanding book by Jim McKeever deals almost entirely with the third stage of Christian life, the overcomer stage, The author feels that it is likely the most important book that he will ever write. In each of Christ's letters to the seven churches in the book of Revelation, special rewards are promised to the overcomers.

A term in the New Testament that is equal to "overcomer" is "bondslave" of Jesus Christ. This book explains what a bondslave is and how one becomes a bondslave of Christ.

It is widely believed that the bride of Christ spoken of the Scriptures includes all Christians. It is possible that the bride of Christ includes only the overcomers; this book examines both sides of that question. Since it is certain that the overcomers are a part of the bride of Christ, and since the Bible says that the overcomers will never leave the temple of God in New Jerusalem, we have a further motivation for wanting to become overcomers. However, the ultimate motivation for the Christian to move into the realm of the overcomer and bondslave is found in the final chapter entitled "The Key To It All." Don't miss this incredible book.

The softback edition of this is $6.95. If you wish a copy, you can use the handy order form on the last page of this book.

ADDITIONAL BOOKS
BY DR. ROBERT THOMPSON

THE FEASTS OF THE LORD

The Bible types represented by the seven holy convocations of Israel are deeply meaningful to the Christian, and yet most Christians are not that familiar with them. These seven convocations are grouped into three major feasts:

1. The Feast of the Passover
2. The Feast of Pentecost
3. The Feast of Tabernacles

The author explains how Christians experience the Feast of the Passover when they receive Jesus Christ. They experience the Feast of Pentecost when they are filled or baptized with the Holy Spirit. God desires to take Christians beyond this point to an even deeper walk with Himself. He wants each of us to go on to the Feast of Tabernacles which is the realm of the overcomers.

OUR LAND IS OCCUPIED: WE MUST INVADE

This is an outstanding book based on the conquest of the promised land by Joshua and the children of Israel. Just as the promised land was occupied and they had to fight, under God's guidance, for actual possession of their inheritance, we, as the body of Christ, will have to fight for possession of our inheritance.

This book presents God's strategy for a victorious spritual warfare. It tells how to enter into inner purity and supernatural power for both the war and effective service in the normal Christian life.

HOW TO GET THESE BOOKS

Each of these books is $5.95 each. Please use the handy order form on the last page to get your copy.

RESPONSE PAGE

Use the other side of this page to obtain materials available from Dr. Thompson and Mr. McKeever. Please record your comments below and then remove this page and mail it in.

COMMENTS:

Attach
Here

Place
Stamp
Here

TO:
OMEGA PUBLICATIONS
P.O. BOX 4130
MEDFORD, OR 97501

Fold Here

NAME________________________________ PHONE______________

ADDRESS____

CITY________________________STATE________ZIP______________

Gentlemen:

I am enclosing a check (payable to Omega Publications) for:

☐ $________ for _______softback copies of *YOU CAN OVERCOME* by Jim McKeever at $6.95 each.

☐ $________ for _______softback copies of *THE FEASTS OF THE LORD* by Dr. Robert Thompson at $5.95 each.

☐ $________ for _______softback copies of *OUR LAND OF PROMISE IS OCCUPIED: WE MUST INVADE* by Dr. Robert Thompson at $5.95 each.

☐ $________ for _______additional softback copies of *WHAT COMES AFTER PENTECOST* by Dr. Robert Thompson at $6.95 each.

$________ TOTAL ENCLOSED

Please send me information on:

☐ Your Christian Newsletter, END-TIMES NEWS DIGEST (END)

☐ Please read the comments on the other side.